ART OF

NUMBER 003

ARCHITECTURAL
ILLUSTRATION

ROCKPORT

THIS BOOK IS DEDICATED TO THE MEMORY OF ROBERT LAWRENCE McILHARGEY | **1942–1998**

One of North America's best-loved and most highly respected architectural Illustrators, Bob McIlhargey was also an accomplished designer and inveterate traveler,
photographer, outdoorsman, and raconteur. His presence is missed by all who knew him or were touched by his work. His wife and collaborator, Lori Brown,
continues the practice Bob founded.

NUMBER 003

ART OF ARCHITECTURAL
ILLUSTRATION

GLOUCESTER MASSACHUSETTS

EDITED BY *Gordon Grice*

ROCKPORT PUBLISHERS

First published in the United States of America by
Rockport Publishers, Inc.
33 Commercial Street
Gloucester, Massachusetts 01930-5089
Telephone: (978) 282-9590
Facsimile: (978) 283-2742

Distributed to the book trade and art trade in the United States by
North Light Books, an imprint of
F & W Publications
1507 Dana Avenue
Cincinnati, Ohio 45207
Telephone: (800) 289-0963

Other distribution by
Rockport Publishers, Inc.
33 Commercial Street
Gloucester, Massachusetts 01930-5089

ISBN 1-56496-591-0

10 9 8 7 6 5 4 3 2 1

Design: Leeann Leftwich
Front cover images: Mark Nelson, (top);
Lori Brown, (below left); Stephan Hoffpauir (below right)
Back cover image: Angelo DeCastro

Printed in China.

TABLE OF CONTENTS

INTRODUCTION

A NEW AGE OF DISCOVERY BY GORDON GRICE

Drawing is an ancient pursuit. People have been drawing for at least twenty thousand years. The cave drawings in France and Spain are that old. Some drawings in Australia are thought to be even older. Architecture, depending on how you define it, has not been around quite so long—maybe a few thousand years (remember, these drawings are on the walls of caves—nobody knew how to build anything, but they knew how to draw). It was only about five hundred years ago that architecture and drawing finally converged, and architectural drawing was born.

The fifteenth century was an extraordinary time. Humanity's knowledge of itself and the universe it inhabited began to expand at an incredible rate. Among the many intellectual achievements of the age can be counted the introduction of orthographic architectural drawing (that is, floor plans, building elevations, and so on, traditionally ascribed to Leon Battista Alberti, ca. 1435) and resolution of the rules of linear perspective (Filippo Brunelleschi, ca. 1415). At last, architects could sketch out scaled representations of their proposed creations, illusions of form and space itself that could be understood by anyone, before they were built, and even draw realistic views. Not coincidentally, the great expansion of the fifteenth century also had a physical component: the beginning of the age of navigation, the discovery of unknown continents, and extension of the boundaries of the familiar world.

Now, five hundred years later, we find ourselves in a new age of discovery, one whose theme is not expansion but contraction. To discover the origins of our vast universe, we study the behavior of subatomic particles. The sum of our knowledge has been codified into binary digits and shrunk onto microchips. A simple office computer can hold within it all the rules of architectural drawing—orthographic and perspective. We may be the last generation that knows or understands these elegant rules. All we need to do now is push the buttons.

With the contraction and reduction of all that is familiar, there is a corresponding sense of contraction of the world in which we live. Renaissance navigators sailed into the vast unknown. Today, you can speak to someone half a world away by picking up a cell phone and hitting "auto dial." Sending documents? A courier will have them there in a few days at most. Can't wait? Send a fax. Send an e-mail. More than any other factors, the twin phenomena of the digital revolution and the shrinking world have affected the art of architectural illustration. In the pages that follow, you will find ample evidence of this. Some examples are obvious, others quite subtle, but the change is profound and ongoing.

DIGITAL VERSUS MANUAL, MOUSEPAD VERSUS SKETCHPAD

Digital used to mean "with the use of the fingers." I have a "digital piano" at my house. What other kind is there?

Digital is now a way of reducing every conceivable thought or activity to a binary code of ones and zeroes (digits). Qualities can now be constructed as quantities. The formulas for these conversions are very complicated, and powerful computers are required. Without the intervention of a sound human mind, however, the result is not always pleasing. In the art world, we were a lot better off with the old definition of digital.

In technical illustration, especially architectural illustration, precision and accuracy are valued to a degree. Thus, a technology that promises precision at the touch of a button, not to mention speed, versatility, and an unbelievable world of choices and options, is bound to be seen as a blessing. However, as Willem van den Hoed points out in his essay, aesthetic considerations are paramount. Here, the human mind—the analog, not digital, computer—still has the advantage.

Digital drawings are not always "gee-whiz" drawings. On the pages of this book, there are many more examples of the use of computers in drawing than even a trained eye can discern. The following is a short list of the many ways in which computers are commonly used in generating architectural drawings:

1. Digital model (DM), hand-rendered;

2. DM, rendered with a rendering program (off-the-shelf or custom);

3. DM, rendered with a paint program;

4. Hand-done rough, scanned and digitally rendered;

5. Digitally drawn, not using a modeling program, rendered digitally, manually, or both;

6. Digital or manual rough drawing or model, rendered manually and manipulated with a digital paint program; and

7. Animations and pans that may employ any of the preceding configurations.

Of all these scenarios, only the second is referred to universally as "computer drawing" and is instantly recognizable as such. In fact, most architectural drawing today uses computer technology at some stage. If you do not believe that computer drafting has taken over, check the size of the drafting supply section of your local art store—if it still has one.

INTERNATIONAL PRACTICE: DRAWING WITHOUT BORDERS

It sometimes seems as though all the new buildings in the world are designed to look more or less the same. Possibly they are, but the designers who create them are, at the same time, becoming more knowledgeable about the cultures and conditions that prevail in a seemingly infinite number of places. Buildings may appear to have been designed according to a single set of principles, but those principles often have been derived from and modified to accommodate an incalculable number of local requirements and preferences. In his essay, Angelo DeCastro writes that sensitivity to local conditions and tastes—as well as a good knowledge of politics, geography, language, customs, and regulations—is as important for the illustrator as for the beleaguered architect. Contextual sensitivity is the province of artist and architect alike.

David Xiaoping Xu, of Nanjing, China, offers a comprehensive and fascinating description of how the practice of architectural illustration in China differs from that in North America. Since writing this piece, Xiaoping has come to live and work in North America—a testimony to Xiaoping's own adventurous spirit, but owing equally to digital technology and the shrinking-world phenomena. I met Xiaoping in Memphis, Tennessee. Our correspondence began on the Internet. He is now a local call.

As you look through the wealth of images in this book, think of how much and how little has changed in the past five centuries. What is probably most striking is the incredible variety in style and content. Hand-drawn images straight out of the Middle Ages may appear side-by-side with fantastic, non-objective computer drawings. There are perspectives of buildings located around the corner from you and others situated half a world away. I think Alberti and Brunelleschi would be impressed. Architectural illustrators are the contemporary custodians of the perspective legacy, and it appears to be in good hands.

JAMES AKERS

AKERS DESIGN RENDER 314 MAIN STREET GREAT BARRINGTON, MASSACHUSETTS 01230 413.528.9018 TEL 413.528.9145 FAX
HTTP://WWW.AKERSDESIGNRENDER.COM

Akers Design Render offers a range of rendering and design consulting services. The studio is located in the Berkshires of Southwestern Massachusetts, two and a half hours from both New York and Boston, and forty-five minutes from the Albany airport. James Akers worked for ten years as a designer with a number of top firms before becoming a full-time renderer in 1989. He is a registered architect with advanced degrees in architecture and real-estate development.

In addition to traditional rendering in watercolor and pencil, Akers has become increasingly involved in collaborating with architects and designers to develop their ideas in quick, in-house sketches and renderings. His work has been honored with awards in both architecture and illustration, and has been featured prominently in the annual shows of both the American Society of Architectural Perspectivists and the New York Society of Renderers.

ABOVE
PROJECT
Proposed Media Tower
ARCHITECT
Rockwellgroup Architects
New York, New York
RENDERING SIZE
6" x 10" (15 cm x 25 cm)
MEDIUM
Pencil, photocopy, and collage

LEFT
PROJECT
Istanbul Cultural Center
Istanbul, Turkey
ARCHITECT
Skidmore, Owings & Merrill Architects
RENDERING SIZE
18" x 18" (46 cm x 46 cm)
MEDIUM
Watercolor

OPPOSITE
PROJECT
Study for Copperfield Restaurant
ARCHITECT
Rockwellgroup Architects
New York, New York
RENDERING SIZE
12" x 18" (30 cm x 46 cm)
MEDIUM
Watercolor and Photoshop collage

PROJECT
Private Residence
Long Island, New York

ARCHITECT
Peter Marino

RENDERING SIZE
30" x 12" (76 cm x 30 cm)

MEDIUM
Watercolor

ABOVE

PROJECT
Olympic Baseball Venue for 2000 Olympics
Istanbul, Turkey

ARCHITECT
Stang Newdow Architects
Atlanta, Georgia

RENDERING SIZE
12" x 18" (30 cm x 46 cm)

MEDIUM
Watercolor

LEFT

PROJECT
Proposal for Coors Field, Denver Colorado

ARCHITECT
Rockwellgroup Architects
New York, New York

RENDERING SIZE
8" x 10" (20 cm x 25 cm)

MEDIUM
Ink and colored pencil

PROJECT
Banco Santander

ARCHITECT
Clark Tribble Harris Lee Architects

RENDERING SIZE
14" x 20" (36 cm x 51 cm)

MEDIUM
Pencil

BELOW
PROJECT
Academy Awards Theater

ARCHITECT
Rockwellgroup Architects
New York, New York

RENDERING SIZE
16" x 8" (41 cm x 20 cm)

MEDIUM
Pencil

BELOW
PROJECT
Proposal for Battersea Power Station
London, England

ARCHITECT
Rockwellgroup Architects
New York, New York

RENDERING SIZE
16" x 6" (41 cm x15 cm)

MEDIUM
Pencil and collage

PROJECT
Proposed Residential Towers
Columbus, Ohio

ARCHITECT
Gwathmey Siegel Architects

RENDERING SIZE
12" x 16" (30 cm x 41 cm)

MEDIUM
Watercolor over wireframe

12

RIGHT

PROJECT
City University of New York (CUNY)
Graduate School Dining
New York, New York

ARCHITECT
Gwathmey Siegel Architects

RENDERING SIZE
12" x 16" (30 cm x 41 cm)

MEDIUM
Watercolor over wireframe

RIGHT

PROJECT
City University of New York (CUNY)
Graduate School Lobby
New York, New York

ARCHITECT
Gwathmey Siegel Architects

RENDERING SIZE
12" x 16" (30 cm x 41 cm)

MEDIUM
Watercolor over wireframe

LEFT

PROJECT
Competition for Hamburg Waterfront
Hamburg, Germany

ARCHITECT
Skidmore, Owings & Merrill Architects

RENDERING SIZE
8" x 20" (20 cm x 51 cm)

MEDIUM
Watercolor over wireframe

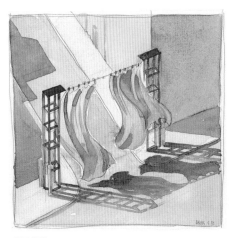

PROJECT
Proposal for 5th Avenue
New York, New York

ARCHITECT
Rockwellgroup Architects
New York, New York

RENDERING SIZE
4" x 4" (10 cm x 10 cm)

MEDIUM
Watercolor

PROJECT
Competition Proposal for Gulf Western Tower
New York

ARCHITECT
Moed de Armas
New York, New York

RENDERING SIZE
12" x 16" (30 cm x 41 cm)

MEDIUM
Watercolor

MANUEL AVILA
WITH PETER JABLOKOW

3700 LAKE SHORE DRIVE, NO. 109   CHICAGO, ILLINOIS 60613   773-404-0798 TEL   773-404-0799 FAX

Manuel Avila and Peter Jablokow have been working together for more than eight years. They have come to believe that, despite the fact that the process, mechanics, and marketing procedures of the business of architectural illustration have changed dramatically, the ultimate goal is still an artist's rendering of a design project.

A successful rendering requires a good deal of thought and care. Manuel Avila has developed a technique that considers the environmental and contextual elements as well as the design details of a project. People, landscaping, vehicles, and other entourage items are rendered with attention to detail to create a realistic image. The result is a professional representation of the project in the real world.

A typical rendering is first done in black and white and is then reproduced in full color. In this way, the client has the opportunity to review and accept two illustrations: one in black and white for newspapers and other publications and the other in color for display and for presentations.

PROJECT
PABT Competition
New York, New York

ARCHITECT
Hellmuth, Obata + Kassabaum
New York, New York

This office tower and retail complex would be located at the bus terminal in busy midtown Manhattan.

PETER JABLOKOW

ABOVE LEFT
PROJECT
Trinity High School
Trinity Valley, Texas

ARCHITECT
Perkins & Will
Chicago, Illinois

RENDERING SIZE
11" x 15" (28 cm x 38 cm)

MEDIUM
Watercolor

This educational building with Spanish flavor is set on a sloping site that allows for the creation of courtyards like this one.

ABOVE RIGHT
PROJECT
House on a Hill No. 2

ARCHITECT
Peter Jablokow
Chicago, Illinois

RENDERING SIZE
9" x 9" (23 cm x 23 cm)

MEDIUM
Colored pencil

This fantasy design, set in the mountains, is part of a series of imaginary houses in dreamy sites.

RIGHT
PROJECT
Restaurant in Saudi Arabia
Jeddah, Saudi Arabia

ARCHITECT
McClier Corporation
Chicago, Illinois

This interior has an abundance of Western flavor, set in the city of Jeddah.

RENDERING SIZE
11" x 12" (28 cm x 30 cm)

MEDIA
Mixed

BELOW RIGHT
PROJECT
Suburban House
near Chicago, Illinois

RENDERING SIZE
10" x 13" (25 cm x 33 cm)

MEDIUM
Watercolor

This depiction of an already existing house was commissioned by a client who wanted to remember his first house.

LEFT
PROJECT
Dique 3
São Paolo, Brazil

ARCHITECT
Hellmuth, Obata + Kassabaum
Dallas, Texas

RENDERING SIZE
11.5" x 12.5" (29 cm x 32 cm)

MEDIA
Mixed

This proposed two-tower complex is set to be developed next to the green preserve by the Atlantic.

BELOW LEFT
PROJECT
Suzhou Tower
Suzhou, China

ARCHITECT
Lohan Associates
Chicago, Illinois

RENDERING SIZE
7" x 10" (18 cm x 25 cm)

MEDIA
Mixed

This is the cornerstone of the development project that was planned to reconfigure this city.

BELOW RIGHT
PROJECT
Dahka International
Karachi, Pakistan

ARCHITECT
Lohan Associates
Chicago, Illinois

RENDERING SIZE
9" x 15" (23 cm x 38 cm)

MEDIA
Mixed

This view shows a complex including a hotel and office, retail, and parking space that is intended to revive the business district.

RIGHT

PROJECT
Samaritano Hospital Addition
Brazil

ARCHITECT
Hellmuth, Obata + Kassabaum
Houston, Texas

RENDERING SIZE
10" x 16" (25 cm x 41 cm)

MEDIA
Mixed

This proposed expansion, which includes
a parking deck, serves as a base for the
access road.

BELOW RIGHT

PROJECT
Museum of Natural Sciences
Chicago, Illinois

ARCHITECT
Perkins & Will
Chicago, Illinois

RENDERING SIZE
8" x 16" (20 cm x 41 cm)

MEDIA
Mixed

Surrounded by a park and landscaped, this
bird's-eye view shows the future museum in
Lincoln Park.

OPPOSITE

PROJECT
Lakeside Square
Chicago, Illinois

ARCHITECT
Lucien Lagrange and Associates
Chicago, Illinois

RENDERING SIZE
8.5" x 20" (22 cm x 51 cm)

MEDIA
Mixed

This proposed project would fill vacant land
with nine million square feet (836,000 square
meters) of office, hotel, residential, and
retail space.

LEFT

PROJECT
Tonti-Peck School
Chicago, Illinois

ARCHITECT
Knight Architects
Chicago, Illinois

RENDERING SIZE
9" x 12" (23 cm x 31 cm)

MEDIA
Mixed

Mixing a conceptual view with a real courtyard,
this illustration shows a floor plan combined
with a three-dimensional courtyard.

BELOW LEFT

PROJECT
Bridge over Des Plaines River
Des Plaines, Illinois

ARCHITECT
McDonough Architects
Chicago, Illinois

RENDERING SIZE
14.5" x 24" (37 cm x 61 cm)

MEDIA
Mixed

A concrete bridge structure, one of two
alternatives, shown in early autumn.

ABOVE LEFT
PROJECT
Acropolis
Santo Domingo, Dominican Republic
ARCHITECT
VOA Associates, Inc.
Chicago, Illinois
RENDERING SIZE
10" x 14" (25 cm x 36 cm)
MEDIA
Mixed

This interior view of a shopping center calls to mind the structural wood of an old ship.

ABOVE
PROJECT
Bond Link
Shanghai, China
ARCHITECT
Skidmore, Owings & Merrill Architects
Chicago, Illinois
RENDERING SIZE
11.5" x 15" (29 cm x 38 cm)
MEDIA
Mixed

This atrium view allows a look at all the retail floors at their busiest time of the day.

LEFT
PROJECT
Lopez Centre
Manila, Philippines
ARCHITECT
Skidmore, Owings & Merrill Architects
Chicago, Illinois
RENDERING SIZE
14" x 21" (36 cm x 53 cm)
MEDIA
Mixed

The lobby of this office tower meets the challenge of dramatizing a space with similar materials and finishes.

BELOW LEFT
PROJECT
Chicago Police Department Headquarters
Chicago, Illinois
ARCHITECT
OWP&P Architects
Chicago, Illinois
RENDERING SIZE
11" x 17" (28 cm x 43 cm)
MEDIA
Mixed

This lobby view of police headquarters shows a convention hall, a small theater, and offices for the public.

LEFT

PROJECT
301 South Wacker Drive
Chicago, Illinois

ARCHITECT
Skidmore, Owings & Merrill Architects
Chicago, Illinois

RENDERING SIZE
10" x 22.5" (25 cm x 57 cm)

MEDIA
Mixed

This proposed tower in the downtown area is scheduled to be completed by 2001.

PROJECT
Musee Plaza
Beirut, Lebanon

ARCHITECT
Perkins & Will
Chicago, Illinois

RENDERING SIZE
13" x 22.5" (33 cm x 57 cm)

MEDIA
Mixed

This drawing was created for a competition; the resulting retail and office tower could have been the tallest in the city.

RICHARD C. BAEHR

305 NORTHERN BOULEVARD GREAT NECK, NEW YORK 11021 516-466-0470 TEL 516-466-1670 FAX

Richard Baehr is an architect who specializes in architectural rendering. Occasionally using pencil or other media, Baehr mostly produces photo-realistic tempera renderings in response to client demand for the powerful expression of design ideas. Moreover, tempera has the unique advantage of allowing changes or additions when necessary.

Baehr has exhibited his work in the United States, Canada, Europe, and Asia and has lectured in New York, Boston, Toronto, and Osaka. He is a graduate of the Cooper Union School of Architecture and the University of Cincinnati School of Applied Arts. He is a member of the American Institute of Architects, the American Society of Architectural Perspectivists, and the New York Society of Renderers. His book, *Architectural Rendering in Tempera*, was published in 1995 by John Wiley & Sons.

ABOVE
PROJECT
445 Park Avenue, Rehabilitation of Ground Floor and Entrance
New York, New York

ARCHITECT
Der Scutt Architect
New York, New York

RENDERING SIZE
18.25" x 15" (46.5 cm x 38 cm)

MEDIUM
Tempera

LEFT
PROJECT
Office Building Rehabilitation
White Plains, New York

ARCHITECT
Perkins & Will
New York, New York

RENDERING SIZE
29.625" x 16.5" (75.5 cm x 42 cm)

MEDIUM
Tempera

PROJECT
General Motors Building, Facade Rehabilitation
New York, New York

CLIENT
Donald J. Trump

RENDERING SIZE
16" x 34" (41 cm x 86 cm)

MEDIUM
Tempera

21

LEFT
PROJECT
World Trade Center Phase I
Xiamen, China

CLIENT
Cannon Architects
New York, New York

RENDERING SIZE
30" x 24" (76 cm x 61 cm)

MEDIUM
Tempera

BELOW LEFT
PROJECT
World Trade Center Phase II
Xiamen, China

CLIENT
Cannon Architects
New York, New York

RENDERING SIZE
30" x 24" (76 cm x 61 cm)

MEDIUM
Tempera

This second tower was added to the original
after the reproduction of Phase I.

PROJECT
Casino Yacht

CLIENT
Donald J. Trump

RENDERING SIZE
31.5" x 16" (80 cm x 41 cm)

MEDIUM
Tempera

TOP LEFT

PROJECT
Trump World Tower
New York, New York

CLIENT
Donald J. Trump

ARCHITECT
Costas Kondylis & Associates

RENDERING SIZE
15.375" x 34" (39 cm x 85 cm)

MEDIUM
Tempera

TOP RIGHT

PROJECT
345 Hudson Street,
Rehabilitation of Building Entrance
New York, New York

CLIENT
Berg and Forster
New York, New York

RENDERING SIZE
19" x 15.5" (48 cm x 39 cm)

MEDIUM
Tempera

PROJECT
Proposed New York Stock Exchange Building
New York, New York

CLIENT
Donald J. Trump

ARCHITECT
Kohn, Pedersen, Fox Associates, PC
New York, New York

RENDERING SIZE
37.5" x 19" (95 cm x 48 cm)

24

ABOVE

PROJECT
Lang Suan Ville
Bangkok, Thailand

CLIENT
Frank Williams and Associates
New York, New York

RENDERING SIZE
19.5" x 37" (50 cm x 94 cm)

MEDIUM
Tempera

ABOVE RIGHT

PROJECT
Trump International Hotel and Tower
New York, New York

CLIENT
Donald J. Trump

ARCHITECT
Philip Johnson, Ritchie and Fiore
New York, New York

RENDERING SIZE
16" x 33" (41 cm x 84 cm)

MEDIUM
Tempera

BELOW

PROJECT
Piarco International Airport
Trinidad

CLIENT
Birk / Hillman
Miami, Florida

RENDERING SIZE
40" x 22" (102 cm x 56 cm)

MEDIUM
Tempera

BELOW

515 Park Avenue
New York, New York

Frank Williams and Associates
New York, New York

15.75" x 32.5" (40 cm x 83 cm)

Tempera

Japan Rail Central Tower
Nagoya, Japan

Kohn, Pedersen, Fox Associates, P.C.
New York, New York

18" x 9.5" (46 cm x 24 cm), 18" x 11" (46 cm
x 28 cm), 15.5" x 8.25" (39 cm x 20.5 cm),
18" x 9.5" (46 cm x 24 cm)

Tempera

FRANK BARTUS

FRANK BARTUS   225 SOUTH SWOOPE AVENUE, SUITE 205   MAITLAND, FLORIDA 32751   407-539-2606 TEL   407-644-7901 FAX
www.genesisstudios.com   info@genesisstudios.com

The primary objective of the staff of Genesis Studios is to explore with clients the nuances of their design and their feelings about its expression.

"I would like to thank you for the hard work and long hours you have put into this project. The Project Team leaves for Japan on Monday, June 22, to present the entire conceptual package, and they are thoroughly pleased to have your piece as the main overview of the park."—Merrill L. Puckett, Director of Creative Development/Brand Management, Paramount Parks

"The quality of the rendering not only clearly conveyed our design concept to the city but established a perceived quality level of our company that was many levels above our competition."—Edward L. Schrank, President, Welbro Development, Inc.

"Would I recommend Genesis Studios to you? Certainly!"—R. Matz, AIA

PROJECT
Gables on the Green
Coral Gables, Florida
CLIENT
Roger International
ARCHITECT
Fullerton Diaz Architects, Inc.
Miami, Florida
MEDIUM
Gouache

PROJECT
Twilight Study
MEDIUM
Gouache

BELOW
PROJECT
M. D. Anderson Cancer Center
Orlando, Florida
ARCHITECT
Rogers, Lovelock & Fritz, Inc.
MEDIUM
Gouache

27

PROJECT
MGM Grand Casino
Detroit, Michigan
CLIENT
MGM Grand Development, Inc.
ARCHITECT
Wimberly, Allison, Tong & Goo
Newport Beach
MEDIUM
Gouache

LEFT
PROJECT
Capital Plaza
Orlando, Florida
CLIENT
Highwoods Properties
ARCHITECT
Butler, Lemons, Romero
MEDIA
Gouache on photo of existing site

PROJECT
Aventura Mall
Aventura, Florida

CLIENTS
Turnberry Associates
Simon/DeBartolo Properties

ARCHITECT
RTKL Associates
Baltimore, Maryland

MEDIUM
Gouache

RIGHT
PROJECT
Orange County Convention Center
Orlando, Florida

ARCHITECT
Hellman, Hurley, Charvat,
Peacock/Architects, Inc.
Orlando, Florida

MEDIA
Gouache on photo of existing site

BELOW LEFT
PROJECT
Marina and Views at Baypointe
St. Augustine, Florida

ARCHITECT
Fugleberg, Koch Architects
Orlando, Florida

MEDIUM
Gouache

BOTTOM LEFT
PROJECT
Broward County Arena
Broward County, Florida

CLIENT
Harris, Drury & Cohen

ARCHITECT
Ellerbe Beckett
Kansas City, Missouri

MEDIA
Gouache on airbrush-enhanced photo print

29

LEFT
PROJECT
Capital One
Tampa, Florida

ARCHITECT
Hellmuth, Obata + Kassabaum
Tampa, Florida

MEDIUM
Gouache

BELOW LEFT
PROJECT
Hotel Complex
Cartegena, Colombia

ARCHITECT
VOA Associates, Inc.
Chicago, Illinois; Orlando, Florida

MEDIA
Gouache on airbrush-enhanced photo print

ABOVE
PROJECT
Proposed Office Tower
ARCHITECT
Hellmuth, Obata + Kassabaum
Tampa, Florida
MEDIUM
Watercolor

OPPOSITE
PROJECT
Olympian Place
Manila, Philippines
ARCHITECT
Hellman, Hurley, Charuat,
Peacock/Architects, Inc.
MEDIUM
Computer-generated

RIGHT
PROJECT
Orlando International Airport,
Proposed Concourse Improvements
Orlando, Florida
ARCHITECT
ZHA
MEDIUM
Watercolor

BELOW RIGHT
PROJECT
Hammock Beach
Palm Coast, Florida
CLIENT
The Ginn Company
DESIGN CONCEPT
Genesis Studios, Inc.
MEDIA
Watercolor

ABOVE
PROJECT
Avatar
Poinciana, Florida
ARCHITECT
Spillis, Candela & Partners, Inc.
MEDIUM
Watercolor

31

LORI BROWN

McILHARGEY/BROWN ASSOCIATES   1639 WEST 2ND AVENUE, #410   VANCOUVER, BRITISH COLUMBIA V6J 1H3   CANADA
604-736-7897 TEL   604-736-9763 FAX   EMAIL MCILBROWN@YAHOO.COM

McIlhargey/Brown Associates has worked since 1980 on various projects, including resorts, theme attractions, world's fairs, waterfront redevelopments, city planning, and other residential and commercial projects.

The firm participates as a team with architects, developers, and clients to represent projects using a mixed-media technique.

As members of American Society of Architectural Perspectivists (ASAP) since 1987, Lori Brown and Bob McIlhargey have won numerous awards and have been featured in various architectural publications.

ABOVE
PROJECT
Banff Redevelopment Project
Banff, Alberta, Canada
ARCHITECT
Design Workshop
Aspen, Colorado

Landplan Associates
Calgary, Alberta, Canada
RENDERING SIZE
8" x 12" (20 cm x 30 cm)
MEDIUM
Pen and ink

PROJECT
Melaka Educational City
Melaka, Malaysia
ARCHITECT
Arthur Erickson • Atelier Architects
Vancouver, British Columbia, Canada
RENDERING SIZE
20" x 25" (51 cm x 76 cm)
MEDIA
Mixed

PROJECT
Theme Park
Durban, South Africa

CLIENT
Forrec, Ltd
Toronto, Ontario, Canada

RENDERING SIZE
25" x 40" (64 cm x 102 cm)

MEDIA
Mixed

ABOVE RIGHT
PROJECT
Space Park
Bremen, Germany

ARCHITECT
Architectura Architects
Vancouver, British Columbia, Canada

RENDERING SIZE
25" x 40" (64 cm x 102 cm)

MEDIA
Mixed

RIGHT
PROJECT
Whistler Village
Vancouver, British Columbia, Canada

ARCHITECT
Robert McIlhargey/Architecture

RENDERING SIZE
12" x 15" (30 cm x 38 cm)

MEDIA
Mixed

Whistler Village in Vancouver has been awarded
the Canadian bid for the 2010 Winter Olympics.

BELOW RIGHT
PROJECT
Callaghan Site, Whistler Village
Vancouver, British Columbia, Canada

RENDERING SIZE
12" x 12" (30 cm x 30 cm)

MEDIA
Mixed

34

ABOVE LEFT
PROJECT
Vancouver Portside Presentation Plaza,
Whistler Village
Vancouver, British Columbia, Canada
CLIENT
Greystone Properties, Ltd.
RENDERING SIZE
12" x 15" (30 cm x 38 cm)
MEDIA
Mixed

ABOVE RIGHT
PROJECT
Whistler-Cascade Lodge
Whistler, British Columbia, Canada
ARCHITECT
John Perkins Architect
RENDERING SIZE
20" x 25" (51 cm x 64 cm)
MEDIA
Mixed

LEFT
PROJECT
Whistler Montebello II
Whistler, British Columbia, Canada
RENDERING SIZE
20" x 25" (51 cm x 64 cm)
MEDIA
Mixed

BELOW LEFT
PROJECT
Ocean Park
Bremerhaven, Germany
ARCHITECT
Architectura Architects
Whistler, British Columbia, Canada
RENDERING SIZE
18" x 24" (46 cm x 61 cm)
MEDIA
Mixed

34

ABOVE
PROJECT
Kuwait Waterfront Phase 4
Kuwait City, Kuwait

ARCHITECT
Arthur Erickson • Atelier Architects

RENDERING SIZE
20" x 28" (51 cm x 71 cm)

MEDIA
Mixed

RIGHT AND BELOW RIGHT
PROJECT
Mangaf Beach Resort
Kuwait City, Kuwait

ARCHITECT
Arthur Erickson • Atelier Architects

RENDERING SIZE
12" x 15" (30 cm x 38 cm)

MEDIA
Mixed

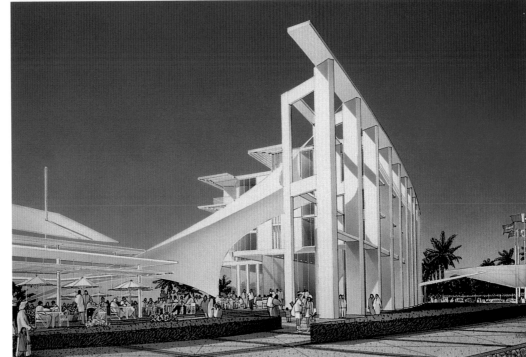

PROJECT
Portside Convention Center
Vancouver, British Columbia, Canada

ARCHITECTS
Arthur Erickson Architectural Corporation
Architectura Architects
Whistler, British Columbia, Canada
Musson Cattell Mackey/Zeidler Roberts
Partnership Architects

RIGHT
PROJECT
Edgewater
Vancouver, British Columbia, Canada

ARCHITECT
Robert Stern

CLIENT
Millennium Development Corp.

RENDERING SIZE
15" x 20" (38 cm x 51 cm)

MEDIA
Mixed

BELOW RIGHT
PROJECT
Great World City
Singapore

ARCHITECT
Perkins & Company Architects

RENDERING SIZE
20" x 20" (51 cm x 51 cm)

MEDIA
Mixed

RIGHT AND BELOW RIGHT
PROJECT
Campbell River Waterfront Redevelopment
Campbell River, British Columbia, Canada
RENDERING SIZE
20" x 25" (51 cm x 64 cm)
MEDIA
Mixed

LEFT
PROJECT
Furry Creek Town Centre
Furry Creek, British Columbia, Canada

ARCHITECT
Design Workshop
Aspen, Colorado

BELOW LEFT
PROJECT
Suter Brook
British Columbia, Canada

CLIENT
Greystone Properties

ARCHITECT
Civitas Urban Design & Planning

RENDERING SIZE
12" x 15" (30 cm x 38 cm)

MEDIA
Mixed

NICHOLAS BUCCALO

THE DRAWING STUDIO   362 DEGRAW STREET   BROOKLYN, NEW YORK 11231   718-488-7894 TEL AND FAX   WWW.DRAWINGSTUDIO.COM

The Drawing Studio specializes in digital illustrations for the information age. At The Drawing Studio, use of the digital medium offers flexibility, speed, and quality. Revisions can be made easily and quickly. The medium lends itself to finding the perfect viewpoint and angle of the sun, and different materials can be "mapped onto" a drawing to see their effect on a design. Quick elevations, sections, and plans can be created effortlessly with exact lighting and textures applied. Each image is saturated with full, rich color, and everyone gets an "original," high-quality Iris print.

ABOVE
PROJECT
Lujiazui-Itochu Office Building, Lobby
Shanghai, China
CLIENT
Sydness Architects, P.C.
New York, New York
RENDERING SIZE
18" x 25" (46 cm x 64 cm)
MEDIUM
Computer-generated
STATUS
Competition winner
Under construction

RIGHT
PROJECT
Lujiazui-Itochu Office Building Tower
Shanghai, China
CLIENT
Sydness Architects, P.C.
New York, New York
RENDERING SIZE
25" x 30" (64 cm x 76 cm)
MEDIUM
Computer-generated
STATUS
Competition winner
Under construction

PROJECT
AirRail: LaGuardia and Kennedy Airports
Light Rail System
New York City and environs, New York

ARCHITECT
Silver Ziskind Architects
New York, New York

CLIENTS
The Port Authorities of New York
and New Jersey

RENDERING SIZE
18" x 28" (46 cm x 71 cm)

MEDIUM
Computer-generated

This interior view shows TWA's Terminal
platform connector.

STATUS
Competition winner in CD's
(Construction Document phase)

TOP LEFT
PROJECT
AirRail: LaGuardia and Kennedy Airports
Light Rail System
New York City and environs, New York

ARCHITECT
Silver Ziskind Architects
New York, New York

CLIENTS
The Port Authorities of New York
and New Jersey

RENDERING SIZE
18" x 28" (46 cm x 71 cm)

MEDIUM
Computer-generated

This interior view shows the TWA
terminal platform.

STATUS
Competition winner in CD's
(Construction Document phase)

PROJECT
AirRail: LaGuardia and Kennedy Airports
Light Rail System
New York City and environs, New York

ARCHITECT
Silver Ziskind Architects
New York, New York

CLIENTS
The Port Authorities of New York
and New Jersey

RENDERING SIZE
20" x 34" (51 cm x 86 cm)

MEDIUM
Computer-generated

This aerial view shows the TWA terminal station.

STATUS
Competition winner in CD's
(Construction Document phase)

39

LEFT
PROJECT
AirRail: LaGuardia and Kennedy Airports
Light Rail System
New York City and environs, New York

ARCHITECT
Silver Ziskind Architects
New York, New York

CLIENTS
The Port Authorities of New York and New Jersey

RENDERING SIZE
18" x 28" (46 cm x 71 cm)

MEDIUM
Computer-generated

Interior view of Howard Beach Station.

STATUS
Competition winner in CD's
(Construction Document phase)

PROJECT
AirRail: LaGuardia and Kennedy Airports
Light Rail System
New York City and environs, New York

ARCHITECT
Silver Ziskind Architects
New York, New York

CLIENTS
The Port Authorities of New York and New Jersey

RENDERING SIZE
20" x 34" (51 cm x 86 cm)

MEDIUM
Computer-generated

Aerial view of Howard Beach Station.

STATUS
Competition winner in CD's
(Construction Document phase)

PROJECT
Hudson River Studios
New York, New York

CLIENT
WPG Development Corporation
New York, New York

RENDERING SIZE
20" x 30" (51 cm x 76 cm)

MEDIUM
Computer-generated

STATUS
Competition winner in CD's
(Construction Document phase)

RIGHT
PROJECT
Yale Club Dining Room
New York, New York

CLIENT
Sidney Gilbert + Partners
New York, New York

RENDERING SIZE
15" x 28" (38 cm x 71 cm)

MEDIUM
Computer-generated

STATUS
Built

BELOW RIGHT
PROJECT
Pulkovo International Airport Terminal
St. Petersburg, Russia

CLIENT
Silver & Ziskind Architects
New York

RENDERING SIZE
20" x 40" (51 cm x 102 cm)

MEDIUM
Computer-generated

ABOVE FROM LEFT TO RIGHT

PROJECT
Hong Ta Hotel
Shanghai, China

CLIENT
Sydness Architects, P.C.
New York, New York

RENDERING SIZE
20" x 29" (51 cm x 74 cm)

MEDIUM
Computer-generated

STATUS
Competition winner
Under construction

PROJECT
New Gotham Condominium
New York, New York

CLIENT
Schuman, Lichtenstein, Claman, Efron Architects
New York, New York

RENDERING SIZE
29" x 44" (74 cm x 112 cm)

MEDIUM
Computer-generated

STATUS
Built

PROJECT
Robert K. Kraft Center for Jewish Student Life,
Columbia University
New York, New York

CLIENT
Gruzen, Samton Architects, Inc.
New York, New York

RENDERING SIZE
20" x 27" (51 cm x 69 cm)

MEDIUM
Computer-generated

STATUS
Built

PROJECT
31 West 52nd Street Lobby
New York, New York

CLIENTS
Hines, Inc.
New York, New York
K. Roche/J. Dinkeloo Architects
New Haven, Connecticut

RENDERING SIZE
18" x 24" (46 cm x 61 cm)

MEDIUM
Computer-generated

STATUS
Built

PROJECT
Prudential Insurance Corporate Headquarters,
Breakout Space

CLIENT
Swanke, Hayden, Connell Architects
New York, New York

RENDERING SIZE
18" x 28" (46 cm x 71 cm)

MEDIUM
Computer-generated

RIGHT

PROJECT
The Brooklyn Heights Montessori School
Brooklyn, New York

CLIENT
Gruzen, Samton Architects, Inc.
New York, New York

RENDERING SIZE
33" x 45" (84 cm x 114 cm)

MEDIUM
Computer-generated

STATUS
Built

ng Lobby

ology Corridor

rence Room

OPPOSITE

PROJECT
Virtual Reality Walk-Through of IBM's
New Corporate Headquarters
Armonk, New York

CLIENTS
Swanke, Hayden, Connell Architects with
Kohn Pedersen Fox Associates, P.C.
New York, New York

RENDERING SIZE
36" x 49" (91 cm x 124 cm)

MEDIUM
Computer-generated

STATUS
Built

TOP

PROJECT
Club Villa Mugoni
Porto Conte, Alghero, Sardinia

CLIENT
Silver & Ziskind Architects
New York, New York

RENDERING SIZE
24" x 36" (61 cm x 91 cm)

MEDIUM
Computer-generated

STATUS
Under construction

PROJECT
The Pueblo Grande, Reconstruction
Phoenix, Arizona

CLIENT
Archaeology Magazine
New York, New York

RENDERING SIZE
25" x 42" (64 cm x 107 cm)

MEDIUM
Computer-generated

LI CHEN

CYBER EXPRESSION LLC   69-23 173RD STREET   FLUSHING, NEW YORK 11365   718-380-0669 TEL   718-969-5363 FAX

Cyber Expression LLC is an award-winning 3-D visualization firm servicing various establishments, including architectural and interior design firms, real estate developers, and other companies who can utilize computer-generated, three-dimensional, digital models, renderings, and animation.

By using powerful computer systems, Cyber Expression provides a great opportunity for design professionals to bring their design one step closer to reality. Cyber Expression focuses on creating detailed true-scale 3-D geometry, accurate lighting effects, and precise color and texture for materials. Cyber Expression offers quick turn-around time, allowing inevitable design changes that not only reflect the final design work, but also support the design process.

Computer visualization as a new tool and a new media is by far still growing. Cyber Expression is continuously exploring the nature of this new technology to make art and science come alive together and to realize visionary designs.

ABOVE
PROJECT
East Jinjiang Hotel
Shanghai, China
ARCHITECT
Peter Lui Architects

LEFT
PROJECT
Mellon Bank Center
Philadelphia, Pennsylvania
ARCHITECT
Kohn Pedersen Fox Associates P.C.
MEDIUM
Computer-generated (3D Studio)

This project won first prize at the Autodesk International Competition in 1993.

ABOVE

PROJECT
Goldman Sachs Headquarters
London, England

ARCHITECT
Kohn Pedersen Fox Associates P.C.

MEDIUM
Computer-generated (3D Studio)

This project won first prize at the Autodesk
International Competition in 1993.

RIGHT

PROJECT
Mellon Bank Center
Philadelphia, Pennsylvania

ARCHITECT
Kohn Pedersen Fox Associates P.C.

MEDIUM
Computer-generated (3D Studio)

This project won first prize at the Autodesk
International Competition in 1993.

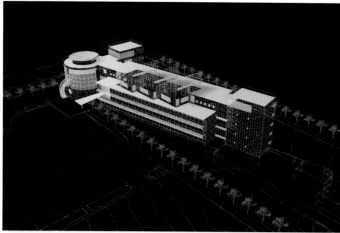

PROJECT
University of Iowa
Iowa

ARCHITECT
Gwathmey Siegel and Associates

MEDIUM
Computer-generated (3D Studio)

BELOW
PROJECT
Zhongshan Avenue South
Nanjing, China

ARCHITECT
Jianxin USA, Inc.

MEDIUM
Computer-generated (3D Studio, Lightscape)

46

PROJECT
200 East 74th Street
New York, New York

ARCHITECT
Environetics Group

MEDIUM
Computer-generated (3D Studio,
Lightscape, Photoshop)

47

PROJECT
Aea Investors, Inc.
New York, New York

ARCHITECT
Keogh Design, Inc.

MEDIUM
Computer-generated (3D Studio, Lightscape)

AWARDS
*Award of Excellence,
Architecture in Perspective 12, 1997*

PROJECT
Kennedy Wilson International
New York, New York

ARCHITECT
Mancini Duffy

MEDIUM
Computer-generated in 3D Studio, Lightscape

48

PROJECT
Ark Asset Management Co.
New York, New York

ARCHITECT
Environetics Group

MEDIUM
Computer-generated (3D Studio, Lightscape)

LEFT
PROJECT
Orient Consumer Credit Pte. Ltd.
Singapore

ARCHITECT
Key International, Inc.

MEDIUM
Computer-generated (3D Studio, Lightscape)

PROJECT
200 East 74th Street
New York, New York

ARCHITECT
Environetics Group

MEDIUM
Computer-generated (3D Studio, Lightscape,
Photoshop)

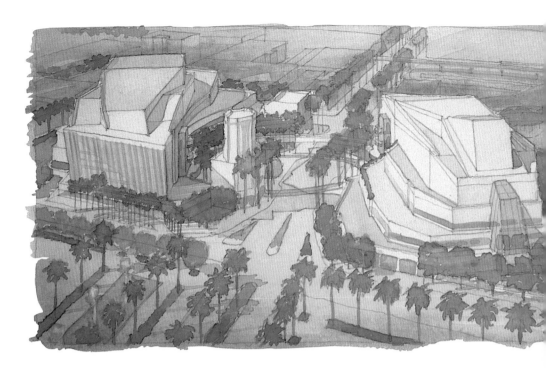

FRANK M. COSTANTINO

F.M. COSTANTINO, INC. 13B PAULINE STREET WINTHROP, MASSACHUSETTS 02152 617-846-4766 TEL 617-846-8720 FAX
WWW.FMCOSTANTINO.COM

With the premise that service to clients is the core of an illustration business, Frank Costantino places special emphasis on the process of creating an image. Given a unique and unusual series of commissions during a two-year collaboration with Cesar Pelli & Associates and the Performing Arts Center Foundation of Greater Miami, Mr. Costantino's process is presented here as a case study of a single, major project that describes both design and drawing decisions that influenced the character of his illustrations.

Subsequent to the selection of Cesar Pelli's winning design, Mr. Costantino was heavily engaged in interpreting the design team's evolving architectural ideas and the Foundation's publicity and fund-raising directives. This partially representative selection of view studies, line layouts, sketches, and final paintings or drawings provides documentation of the methodology typical of Frank Costantino's perspectives.

All of the images in this section depict the Miami Performing Arts Center, Miami, Florida, and the architect for the project's building and spaces is Cesar Pelli & Associates, New Haven, Connecticut. Depending on whether the Foundation or Cesar Pelli was the client of record, the presentation objectives and art direction varied widely, resulting in an explorative process of media and technique.

ABOVE
PROJECT
North Aerial View
RENDERING SIZE
5.25" x 9.5" (13.5 cm x 24 cm)
MEDIUM
Watercolor on Lana 140 H.P.

At one-quarter the final size, this six-hour study sketch helped in exploring a color strategy and setting the paint palette.

RIGHT
PROJECT
Concert Hall and Orchestra
RENDERING SIZE
10.75" x 7.5" (27 cm x 19 cm)
MEDIUM
Watercolor on Lana 140 C.P.

A very gestural preliminary sketch, from the mid-section of the overall perspective layout, defines a "looseness" of style requested by the client. Note full finished image on subsequent page.

Concurrent with ongoing design changes to major elements of the building that repeatedly modified the final layout, the two pencil studies (drawn over an early view angle) explore day and night scenarios. After completion of the perspective line drawing, the recommended shade and shadow angles, the lobby interiors, and the plaza's paving pattern were painted in during the watercoloring stage. The finished image subsequently was printed in a brochure and also released as a poster.

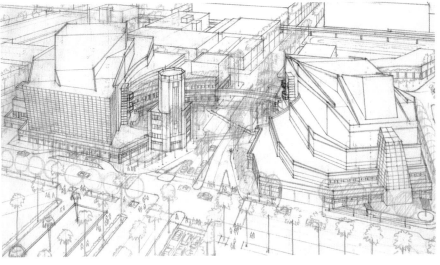

ABOVE LEFT
PROJECT
North Aerial View

RENDERING SIZE
8.25" x 5.5" (20.5 cm x 14 cm)

MEDIUM
Colored pencil on Bienfang paper

To provide the client with comparative study sketches of lighting, this initial impression of an evening setting minimized the volumes of the two buildings.

LEFT
PROJECT
North Aerial View

RENDERING SIZE
4.75" x 6.75" (12 cm x 17 cm)

MEDIUM
Colored pencil on Bienfang paper

The client's preference for this sketch, as an alternative daytime coloration, was the basis for further palette development of the watercolor study on the previous page.

ABOVE
PROJECT
North Aerial View

RENDERING SIZE
8.25" x 14.25" (20.5 cm x 36.5 cm)

MEDIUM
Graphite and colored pencil on vellum

The culmination of many view studies and detailed entourage overlays, the precise final line layout was tightly cropped for tracing onto watercolor paper.

51

BELOW
PROJECT
North Aerial View

RENDERING SIZE
8.5" x 15" (22 cm x 38 cm)

MEDIUM
Watercolor on Lana 140 H.P

Executed at an early schematic design phase, a looser painterly style, with a dramatic afternoon light, helped convey a more engaging first impression of the entire project.

PROJECT
Concert Hall and Orchestra

RENDERING SIZE
10.75" x 16" (27 cm x 41 cm)

MEDIUM
Watercolor on Lana 140 H.P.

Expanding on the color and style of the detail study on the opening page, the full depiction of a concert hall atmosphere, with accents of lighting, was best described from the orchestra's point of view.

BELOW
PROJECT
Ballet/Opera House Hall

RENDERING SIZE
11" x 16.25" (28 cm x 41.5 cm)

MEDIUM
Watercolor on Lana 140 H.P.

For view immediacy of an opera performance, towards a partial staging of *Aida,* this mezzanine angle clearly described the space through a dim, subdued light.

At the schematic design stage of the interior spaces, the Foundation chose a more expressive painting style to convey the desired feel for performances, while still visually appropriate for fund-raising programs.

PROJECT
Concert Hall, Box Suite

RENDERING SIZE
6.5" x 9.75" (17 cm x 25 cm)

MEDIUM
Colored pencil on Bienfang paper

Exactly one year later than the original concert hall interior, a detailed vignette of the more developed design was mandated for a pre-performance setting, wherein the number, gesture, age, ethnicity, and colors of the figures were as important as the box suite itself. Together with five other sketches describing smaller interior spaces, this pencil technique was a visual contrast to the otherwise all watercolor technique of previous images.

BELOW
PROJECT
Ballet/Opera House, Plaza Entry

RENDERING SIZE
9.5" x 12" (24 cm x 30 cm)

MEDIUM
Watercolor on Lana 140 H.P.

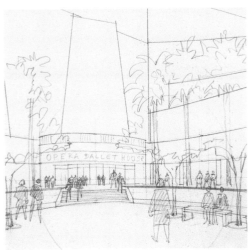

FROM TOP TO BOTTOM
PROJECT
Ballet/Opera House, Plaza Entry

RENDERING SIZE
13.25" x 10.75" (33.5 cm x 27 cm)

MEDIUM
Graphite on trace

PROJECT
Ballet/Opera House, Plaza Entry

RENDERING SIZE
14.75" x 12.5" (38 cm x 32 cm)

MEDIUM
Graphite on trace

PROJECT
Ballet/Opera House, Plaza Entry

RENDERING SIZE
13.25" x 10.5" (33.5 cm x 27 cm)

MEDIUM
Graphite on trace

Quick view blockouts, projected in traditional perspective method, were all completed in one day to provide the architect with a choice of view options for a vignette of a plaza entry.

Prepared in two days, four studies (only three are shown) were laid out in sequence, faxed for client review and input, revised, and finalized to the desired angle. Along with two other images created over three days, this quickly realized sketch of a major plaza entry was executed, in-house, at the architect's office.

PROJECT
South Aerial View

Skyline photo referenced for Layout
© Aerial Photography, Inc.
Fort Lauderdale, Florida

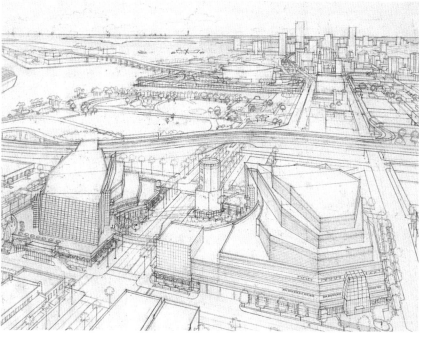

BELOW
PROJECT
Ballet/Opera House, Grand Lobby
RENDERING SIZE
9" x 13.5" (23 cm x 34 cm)
MEDIUM
Watercolor on Lana 140 H.P.

54

Prepared together with the entry view, the enlivening impression of arrival for an evening performance was the premise for describing the defined features of the grand lobby space. The illustrator's overall color scheme was approved by Mr. Pelli, and the architect suggested the transparent finessing of the columns and landscaping. The lighted south aerial view at right shows this lobby area.

PROJECT
South Aerial View
RENDERING SIZE
11.25" x 15" (28.5 cm x 38 cm)
MEDIUM
Graphite and colored pencil on vellum

The important south view—the last and most important image of the project's commissions—set the new complex in the recognizable context of Miami's skyline, harbor, open space, future arena, and proposed millennium tower. After studies were reviewed and the perspective angle was determined, aerial photos similar to this view were provided by the Foundation.

PROJECT
South Aerial View

RENDERING SIZE
6.5" x 8.25" (17 cm x 20.5 cm)

MEDIUM
Watercolor on Lana 140 H.P.

An initial six-hour study addressed the client's visual criteria in a very complex aerial view.

BELOW
PROJECT
South Aerial View

RENDERING SIZE
12.75" x 17" (32 cm x 43 cm)

MEDIUM
Watercolor on Lana 140 H.P.

ABOVE RIGHT
PROJECT
South Aerial View

RENDERING SIZE
6.75" x 9" (17 cm x 23 cm)

MEDIUM
Watercolor on Lana 140 H.P.

At the client's request, a second more unusual atmosphere, featuring interior lighting, was explored in a second study.

To contrast with the earlier north view, and since both the north and south paintings would be shown together often, the Foundation first requested a morning daylight rendering, as shown in the first study. A reassessment of this approach led to the decision to use diffused, late-afternoon daylight for the second study (not an unlikely condition of this southern climate), along with the lighted interiors of each hall.

The project drawings in this portfolio were produced with the expert assistance of Arthur Dutton, M. Planning, Harvard; Michael O'Beirne, B.F.A., M.B.A. Boston University.

ANGELO DeCASTRO

RUA DO ALTO DA MILHA 50-A   2765-297 SÃO JOÃO DO ESTORIL   PORTUGAL   351-1-4671010 TEL   351-1-4661648 FAX
WWW.ADECASTRO.PT   ANGELO@ADECASTRO.PT

Angelo De Castro Architectural Projects and Illustrations was founded in Rio De Janeiro, Brazil, in 1974. Since 1988, De Castro has been residing in Portugal and working exclusively with renderings for architects, engineers, construction companies, and real estate and marketing agencies throughout Europe and Brazil.

To meet the requirements of his clients and prjects, he has developed his drawing techniques in practically all available media, including graphite, PrismaColor, pen and ink, markers, watercolor and airbrush—his speciality. Following the modern trends of graphic arts, he has been elaborating the renderings in the computer and finishing each image with the traditional media. By working on what he calls a "mixed technique" he adds life to the computer images and represents the architecture with all its details and precision.

De Castro is a graduate of Santa Ursula University, Rio De Janeiro, Brazil in Architecture and a member of the Brazilian and Portuguese Architect Association. He has been a member of ASAP—The American Society of Architectural Perspectivists since 1994 and its representative in Portugal. His artwork has been widely exhibited and published in books and magazines in Portugal and abroad.

ABOVE
PROJECT
Spree Forum
Berlin, Germany

CLIENT
Hanseatica Unternehmens Consulting Berlin GmbH
Berlin, Germany

ARCHITECT
Jan and Prof. Josef Paul Kleihues
Berlin, Germany

RENDERING SIZE
16" x 10" (41 cm x 25 cm)

MEDIUM
Airbrush on Schoeller paper

This rendering won an ASAP Award of Distinction at Architecture in Perspective 10 in Seattle, Washington, in 1995.

LEFT
PROJECT
Quartier an der Museumsinsel
Berlin, Germany

CLIENTS
Hanseatica Unternehmens Consulting Berlin GmbH
Berlin, Germany
Deutsche Immobilien Anlagegesellschaft GmbH

ARCHITECTS
Steffen Lehmann & Partner
Berlin, Germany
Arata Isozaki & Associates
Tokyo, Japan

RENDERING SIZE
16" x 8" (41 cm x 20 cm)

MEDIUM
Airbrush on Schoeller paper

This rendering won an ASAP Award of Excellence at Architecture in Perspective 12 in Memphis, Tennessee, in 1997.

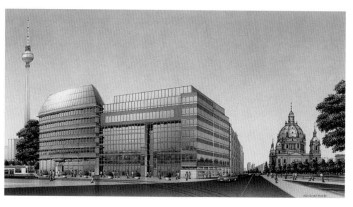

PROJECT
Brazilian Embassy
Berlin, Germany

CLIENT
Deutsche Grundbesitz Management GmbH
Berlin, Germany

RENDERING SIZE
15" x 9" (38 cm x 23 cm)

MEDIUM
Colored pencil on photocopy paper

This rendering won an ASAP Award of
Excellence at Architecture in Perspective 13
in Atlanta, Georgia, in 1998.

PROJECT
São Gabriel Tower, Expo '98
Lisbon, Portugal

CLIENTS
Far Publicidade e Promoções, Ld
Sonae Imobiliaria SA

ARCHITECTS
José Quintela da Fonseca
Lisbon, Portugal
Building Design Partnership
London, England

RENDERING SIZE
16" x 10" (41 cm x 25 cm)

MEDIUM
Airbrush on Schoeller paper

PROJECT
Telecel Building Competition
Lisbon, Portugal

ARCHITECT
Frederico Valsassina Arquitectos, Lda
Lisbon, Portugal

RENDERING SIZE
32" x 20" (81 cm x 51 cm)

MEDIUM
Airbrush on high-gloss paper

PROJECT
Leibniz-kolonnaden
Berlin, Germany

CLIENT
Hanseatica Unternehmens Consulting Berlin GmbH
Berlin, Germany

ARCHITECT
Kollhoff & Timmermann Architekten
Berlin, Germany

RENDERING SIZE
15" x 10" (38 cm x 25 cm)

MEDIUM
Airbrush on Schoeller paper

PROJECT
Office Building
Lisbon, Portugal

CLIENT
Estratégia de Publicidade, Lda

ARCHITECT
Intergaup, Lda
Lisbon, Portugal

RENDERING SIZE
15 "x 11" (38 cm x 28 cm)

MEDIUM
Airbrush on Schoeller paper

BELOW
PROJECT
Hotel-Espada & Bodião
Funchal, Madeira, Portugal

ARCHITECT
Ricardo Nogueira & Associados, Lda
Funchal, Madeira, Portugal

RENDERING SIZE
15" x 11" (38 cm x 28 cm)

MEDIUM
Airbrush on high-gloss paper

FAR LEFT
PROJECT
University of Porto, Faculty of Architecture
Porto, Portugal

ARCHITECT
Álvaro Siza
Porto, Portugal

RENDERING SIZE
5" x 15" (13 cm x 38 cm)

MEDIUM
Airbrush on Schoeller paper

LEFT
PROJECT
Museum of Contemporary Art
Niterói, Brazil

ARCHITECT
Oscar Niemeyer
Rio de Janeiro, Brazil

RENDERING SIZE
5" x 15" (13 cm x 38 cm)

MEDIUM
Airbrush on Schoeller paper

PROJECT
Haus Liebermann-Haus Sommer
Brandenburger Tor
Berlin, Germany

ARCHITECT
Prof. Josef Paul Kleihues
Berlin, Germany

RENDERING SIZE
16" x 10" (41 cm x 25 cm)

MEDIUM
Airbrush on Schoeller paper

ABOVE RIGHT

PROJECT
Wallstrasse Projekt
Berlin, Germany

CLIENT
Hanseatica Unternehmens Consulting
Berlin, Germany

ARCHITECT
PSP—Pysall, Stahrenberg & Partner
Berlin, Germany

RENDERING SIZE
15" x 10" (38 cm x 25 cm)

MEDIUM
Watercolor on Schoeller paper

59

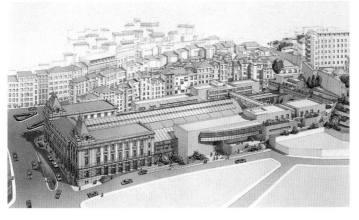

LEFT

PROJECT
São Bento Train Station and Shopping Center
Porto, Portugal

CLIENT
Esbento Sociedade Imobiliaria SA

ARCHITECT
Nuno Leonidas Arquitectos Associados, Lda
Lisbon, Portugal

RENDERING SIZE
15" x 9" (38 cm x 23 cm)

MEDIUM
Airbrush on Schoeller paper

PROJECT
Residential Condominium
Porto, Portugal

ARCHITECT
Ferreira de Almeida Arquitectos, Lda
Porto, Portugal

RENDERING SIZE
16" x 9" (41 cm x 23 cm)

MEDIUM
Airbrush on Schoeller paper

PROJECT
Casa do Alto do Lagoal
Oeiras, Portugal

CLIENT
Portagem Investimento e Promoção Imobiliária,
Lda

ARCHITECT
Álvaro Siza
Porto, Portugal

RENDERING SIZE
5" x 5" (13 cm x 13 cm)

MEDIUM
Airbrush on Schoeller paper

ABOVE LEFT
PROJECT
Residential Condominium
Porto, Portugal

CLIENT
Desigual Marketing e Publicidade, Lda

ARCHITECT
Soarta SA
Porto, Portugal

RENDERING SIZE
16"x 8" (41 cm x 20 cm)

MEDIUM
Airbrush on Schoeller paper

LEFT
PROJECT
Saldanha Residence
Lisbon, Portugal

CLIENT
Imobiliária Fontes Picoas SA

ARCHITECTS
Joao R. Paciência
Lisbon, Portugal
J. Gonzalez Adalid and
Felicisimo Saenz Martinez
Madrid, Spain

RENDERING SIZE
15" x 11" (38 cm x 28 cm)

MEDIUM
Airbrush on Schoeller paper

BELOW LEFT
PROJECT
Lusitânia Cia de Seguros SA
Building Competition
Lisbon, Portugal

ARCHITECT
Frederico Valsassina Arquitectos, Lda
Lisbon, Portugal

RENDERING SIZE
16" x 11" (41 cm x 28 cm)

MEDIUM
Airbrush on Schoeller paper

PROJECT
Casa do Alto do Lagoal (Night)
Oeiras, Portugal

CLIENT
Portagem Investimento e Promoção
Imobiliária, Lda

ARCHITECT
Álvaro Siza
Porto, Portugal

RENDERING SIZE
15" x 5" (38 cm x 13 cm)

MEDIUM
Airbrush on Schoeller paper

PROJECT
Loureshopping
Loures, Portugal

CLIENT
Sonae Imobiliária SA

ARCHITECTS
José Quintela da Fonseca
Lisbon, Portugal
Hellmuth, Obata + Kassabaum
London, England

RENDERING SIZE
16" x 10" (41 cm x 25 cm)

MEDIUM
Airbrush on Schoeller paper

LEE DUNNETTE, AIA

3568 BYRD AVENUE   ALLENTOWN, PENNSYLVANIA 18103   610-776-7427 TEL   610-776-0879 FAX   EMAIL LEEDAIA@FAST.NET

Lee Dunnette brings a sense of magic to the art of architectural illustration. His art transforms the prosaic world of concrete and steel into the ethereal realm of mystery. The mise-en-scène of emotion is his palette.

Dunnette's mastery results from his extensive training and experience. He holds three university degrees and is a member of the AIA, ASAP, and NYSR. He practiced as a registered architect in New York City for ten years and has worked as an architectural illustrator for the last fourteen years. In addition to the traditional techniques, Dunnette is a master at transforming computer rendering into warm, ethereal art.

ABOVE
PROJECT
Astor Plaza, Residential Block
New York, New York
ARCHITECT
Lee Dunnette, AIA
RENDERING SIZE
22" x 22" (56 cm x 56 cm)
MEDIA
Computer-generated, freehand ink, and pastel

BELOW
PROJECT
Buck Center
Marion County, California
ARCHITECT
Pei Cobb Freed & Partners
New York, New York
RENDERING SIZE
23" x 13" (58 cm x 33 cm)
MEDIUM
Acrylic

RIGHT

PROJECT
Petronas Towers, Symphony Hall Entry
Kuala Lumpur, Malaysia

ARCHITECT
Cesar Pelli & Associates
New Haven, Connecticut

RENDERING SIZE
24" x 15" (61 cm x 38 cm)

MEDIUM
Acrylic

BELOW LEFT

PROJECT
Millennium Tower Exterior View
New York, New York

ARCHITECT
KPF Architects/Harvest Communications, Inc.

RENDERING SIZE
12" x 30" (30 cm x 76 cm)

MEDIUM
Acrylic

BELOW MIDDLE

PROJECT
Millennium Tower, Typical Residence
New York, New York

ARCHITECT
KPF Architects/Harvest Communications, Inc.

RENDERING SIZE
12" x 30" (30 cm x 76 cm)

MEDIUM
Acrylic

BELOW RIGHT

PROJECT
Millennium Tower, Public Lobby Details
New York, New York

ARCHITECT
KPF Architects/Harvest Communications, Inc.

RENDERING SIZE
12" x 30" (30 cm x 76 cm)

MEDIUM
Acrylic

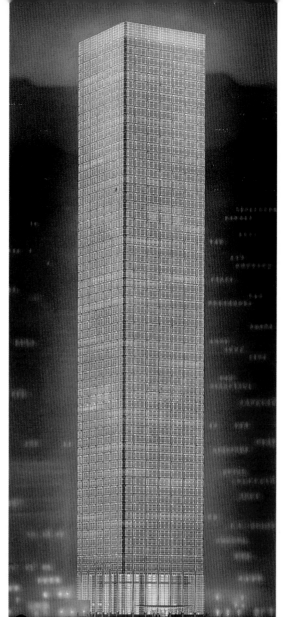

FAR LEFT
PROJECT
Cheung Kong Center (Night Curtainwall Effect)
Hong Kong, China

ARCHITECT
Cesar Pelli & Associates
New Haven, Connecticut

RENDERING SIZE
12" x 30" (30 cm x 76 cm)

MEDIUM
Acrylic

LEFT
PROJECT
Cheung Kong Center (Day Curtainwall Effect)
Hong Kong, China

ARCHITECT
Cesar Pelli & Associates
New Haven, Connecticut

RENDERING SIZE
12" x 30" (30 cm x 76 cm)

MEDIUM
Acrylic

LEFT
PROJECT
Bridgemarket at the 59th Street Bridge
New York, New York

ARCHITECT
Hardy, Holtzman, Pfeiffer Associates
New York, New York

RENDERING SIZE
15" x 12" (38 cm x 30 cm)

MEDIA
Computer-generated, freehand ink

PROJECT
New York-New York Casino triptych
Las Vegas, Nevada

ARCHITECT
Hardy Holtzman Pfeiffer Associates
New York, New York

RENDERING SIZE
11" x 8.5" (28 cm x 22 cm) each

MEDIA
Freehand ink and color wash

LEFT

PROJECT
Port Authority Air Rights Competition
New York, New York

ARCHITECT
Hardy Holtzman Pfeiffer Associates
New York, New York

RENDERING SIZE
22" x 19" (56 cm x 48 cm)

MEDIUM
Pastel

PROJECT
Penn's Landing Triptych
Philadelphia, Pennsylvania

ARCHITECT
Ehrenkrantz, Eckstut & Kuhn, P.C.
New York, New York

RENDERING SIZE
13" x 11" (33 cm x28 cm) each

MEDIUM
Acrylic

RIGHT
PROJECT
E. M. C. Headquarters
Des Moines, Iowa

ARCHITECT
Brooks Borg & Skiles
Des Moines, Iowa

RENDERING SIZE
15" x 23" (38 cm x 58 cm)

MEDIUM
Acrylic

PROJECT
Sloan-Kettering Memorial Hospital Cancer
Center, Visitor's Center
New York, New York

ARCHITECT
Perkins Eastman Architects
New York, New York

RENDERING SIZE
22" x 22" (56 cm x 56 cm)

MEDIA
Freehand ink and color wash

PROJECT
Columbus Circle, 1996 Competition
New York, New York

ARCHITECT
Cesar Pelli & Associates
New Haven, Connecticut

RENDERING SIZE
16" x 23" (41 cm x 58 cm)

MEDIUM
Acrylic

AL FORSTER

P.O. BOX 326   THE SEA RANCH, CALIFORNIA 95497   707-785-2184/800-233-0658 TEL   707-785-2264 FAX

Al Forster has developed his own unique style of architectural presentation, often mixing traditional watercolor and graphite pencil with tonal and textural highlights in colored pencil. All drawings are executed on fully mounted, hand-made watercolor papers that stand alone as self-presentations. His rendered images strike a marvelous balance—literal enough to convey a true sense of proportion and materials, yet loose enough to allow the viewer to partake in and to inhabit the places that are being imagined.

PROJECT
Dragoon Ranch
Southern Arizona

ARCHITECT
Rosendo Gutierrez, Robert York Crockett,
Pace Architects

RENDERING SIZE
11" x 17" (28 cm x 43 cm)

MEDIUM
Watercolor

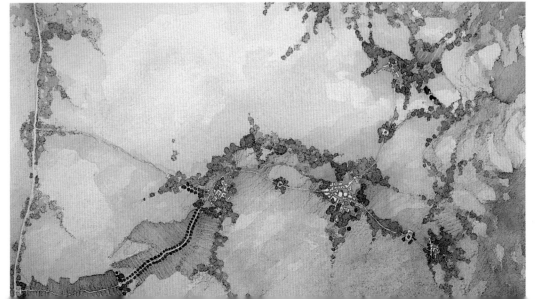

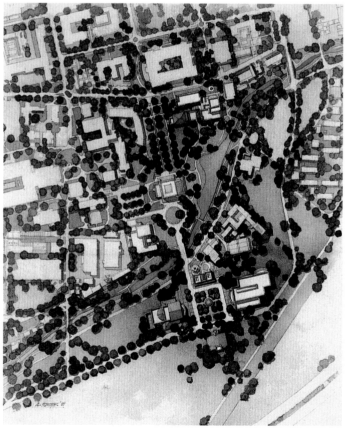

PROJECT
The Aventine, Addition

ARCHITECTS
Original Building: Michael Graves
Princeton, New Jersey
Addition: Carrier-Johnson Architects
San Diego, California

RENDERING SIZE
18" x 24" (46 cm x 61 cm)

MEDIUM
Watercolor

LEFT
PROJECT
University of California at Davis Center
for the Arts

RENDERING SIZE
12" x 18" (30 cm x 46 cm)

MEDIUM
Watercolor

PROJECT
Student Recreation Center

CLIENT
University of California at Irvine

ARCHITECT
Gordon Walker
Seattle, Washington
Langdon Wilson
Newport Beach, California

RENDERING SIZE
15" x 20" (38 cm x 51 cm)

MEDIUM
Watercolor

PROJECT
Rancho Malibu

ARCHITECT
Moore Ruble Yudell
Santa Monica, California

RENDERING SIZE
12"x 18" (30 cm x 46 cm)

MEDIUM
Watercolor

PROJECT
New Town and Resort
Cayman Islands

ARCHITECT
Moore Ruble Yudell
Los Angeles, California

RENDERING SIZE
18" x 20" (46 cm x 51 cm)

MEDIUM
Watercolor

This rendering was a winning entry in
a design competition.

BELOW LEFT
PROJECT
Los Angeles Coliseum, Proposed Remodel
Los Angeles, California

ARCHITECT
Zimmer Gunsul Frasca Partnership
Los Angeles, California

RENDERING SIZE
18" x 24" (46 cm x 61 cm)

MEDIUM
Watercolor

BELOW
PROJECT
Center for Creative Studies
Detroit, Michigan

ARCHITECT
Kohn Pedersen Fox Associates P.C.
New York, New York

RENDERING SIZE
11" x 17" (28 cm x 43 cm)

MEDIUM
Watercolor

PROJECT
University of Virginia, Town Center
Charlottesville, Virginia

ARCHITECT
Mitchel, Matthews & Associates
Charlottesville, Virginia

RENDERING SIZE
14" x 20" (36 cm x 51 cm)

MEDIA
Watercolor and colored pencil

BELOW

PROJECT
Malaysian High Commission
Ottawa, Canada

ARCHITECT
Kaplan McLaughlin Diaz
San Francisco, California

RENDERING SIZE
10" x 15" (25 cm x 38 cm)

MEDIUM
Watercolor

RIGHT

PROJECT
Ciudad Empresarial
Santiago, Chile

ARCHITECTS
Bernardo Urquieta
Renzo Cecchetto
San Francisco, California

RENDERING SIZE
12" x 18" (30 cm x 46 cm)

MEDIUM
Watercolor

FAR RIGHT

PROJECT
Seacastle
Santa Monica, California

ARCHITECT
Killefer Flammang Purtill, Architects
Santa Monica, California

RENDERING SIZE
12" x 18" (30 cm x 46 cm)

MEDIUM
Watercolor

RIGHT

PROJECT
Swanton Pacific Education Center
Santa Cruz, California

ARCHITECT
Austin Design Group
San Diego, California

RENDERING SIZE
15" x 20" (38 cm x 51 cm)

MEDIUM
Watercolor

ARCHITECTURAL ILLUSTRATION IN CHINA

INTERVIEW WITH DAVID XIAOPING XU CONDUCTED BY GORDON GRICE

As mentioned in the Introduction, Xu Xiaoping has been an architectural renderer in both China and North America. A recent discussion with Gordon Grice raised some interesting points about how the profession differs in the two places.

GORDON GRICE: What differences do you see between rendering in China and North America?

DAVID XIAOPING XU: There are quite a few differences. The most apparent is the quality of illustrators. In North America, many illustrators are registered architects and have both strong presentation skills and a rich knowledge of the theories of art and design. Some well-known illustrators have engaged in the profession of architectural illustration and in the practice of architecture for decades, working very hard to enhance their skills. Computer technology in North America is very well developed, but the traditional styles are still playing a leading role in architectural illustrations. Traditional media and styles still have great vitality and are very marketable. In China, illustrators tend to be much younger. Some are college students or graduates. The business of architectural illustration is also young since it depends on the development of the county's economy and building industry. From the mid-1960s to the 1970s, our country was consumed by the "Cultural Revolution." The economy of the country was stagnant and almost collapsed. This, of course, included architecture and the building industry. It was difficult for people outside of China to understand what was really happening during that time. There are still some famous Chinese architects from before the Revolution who are very good at traditional watercolor rendering and pencil drawing, but, as far as I know, only a few of them are rendering professionally now. These architects are graduates of the 1950s whose teachers have studied architecture in Europe and the United States. Unfortunately, it is difficult for the younger generation to see their work.

GG: How large a rendering community is there in China? Are there many full-time, professional renderers?

DXX: It is hard to say exactly how many people are involved in this profession in China, but I believe the community is larger than in any other country in the world. It's impossible to know how many buildings have been built, how many new residential areas have been planned and finished, or how many commercial spaces have been remodeled. Most of these projects probably involve an exterior and an interior perspective for presentation, but we don't know who has done or will do this work. There is no organization like ASAP [The American Society of Architectural Perspectivists] or JARA [the Japanese Architectural Rendering Association] in China. You can't find an illustrator by looking at a members' list or in the yellow pages of a telephone directory. ASAP, for example, with its annual competitions, publications, exhibitions, and other activities, has helped to keep architectural illustrators in communication with one another and has made it easier for them to develop their own styles and techniques. I am glad to be a member of ASAP, which has been an ideal source of information and communication for me. Communication and correspondence among China's illustrators are needed. Although we have an architectural illustration competition and exhibition every three to four years, sponsored by the China Architecture Association, the exhibition is not yet a nationwide traveling show and doesn't include other benefits for illustrators and their clients. The show is only three or four days long, and the participants are usually not invited. We receive a certificate and a catalog and are still alone afterwards.

GG: How does the rendering business operate in China?

DXX: Rendering is a new and growing business in China that is still behind international standards. Illustrators operate as individuals, not as studios. In the eyes of many people, the status of architects is higher than that of illustrators. The legal rights (payment, copyrights, etc.) of illustrators are often not honored.

GG: Who are your clients? How do you get your commissions?

DXX: Since the beginning of my rendering career in 1993, I have been working with the Architectural Design and Research Institute of Southeast University and Nanjing Decoration Construction Engineering Corporation. Most of my clients are architectural design firms and interior design and construction companies. I have also gotten commissions from some real-estate developers. I usually get my commissions by receiving a phone call or a pager message from my client. The conversation you described in the Introduction to *The Art of Architectural Illustration 2* is very familiar to me.

GG: Have computers affected the way you work?

DXX: Very much. Computers have affected every aspect, every corner of the lives of humans. Of course, computers are very efficient tools that can save time and money. I use the computer a lot in setting up 3-D models and generating perspective wireframes. Otherwise, I would have to do it by hand, and that's boring and time-consuming. What is more, the Internet is beginning to change the way we work and communicate. Even while I type this response on my computer, who knows how many renderings are being made? Hundreds? Thousands? The majority of these are certainly computer renderings done by 'computer monkeys' who probably have no architecture, or art and design background. Not to deny the positive role of computer wizards in our rendering community, but rendering is an artistic creation. It is not enough to be good at operating computer software and hardware. A renderer should be a designer or an artist.

GG: Do you have to travel very much within China or abroad?

DXX: Yes, I do. I have traveled many places for my business within China. There are different reasons for this, such as meeting and talking with my clients, inspecting construction sites, or taking photographs. Last year I attended the convention and exhibition of ASAP in Memphis, Tennessee. It was a very good opportunity for me to get to know the work of illustrators from North America and other countries. Although some of the artists' work had been seen in China in printed form, seeing the original works was quite different. During my trip in the United States, I was invited to visit the studios of Mr. Frank Costantino and Mr. Paul Stevenson Oles in Boston, and Mr. Christopher Grubbs in San Francisco. I was very impressed by the unique style and consummate technique of their works. Except for my last trip to the United States in the fall of 1997, I have not been to other countries yet. But I am sure I will have more opportunities to travel abroad in the coming years.

GG: Do you keep in touch with illustrators all over the world? What does this contact mean to you?

DXX: Since ASAP's convention last year I have been in contact with several famous illustrators from the United States and Canada. I am planning to introduce ten to twelve North American illustrators and their works to Chinese readers in a professional magazine called *Interior Design & Construction*. This project has already begun. Today's world is the world of information and communication. To keep in touch with illustrators all over the world means that I am not alone. We can share information and learn from each other.

GORDON GRICE, OAA, FRAIC

65 OLD MILL DRIVE   TORONTO, ONTARIO, CANADA M4G 3W8   416-536-9191 TEL   416-696-8866 FAX

Since 1974, Gordon Grice has served an international clientele from his home base in Toronto, Ontario, Canada. He believes that a good illustration is a working document. An illustrator's job is not merely to make a building look attractive; a good illustration must explain an idea by drawing attention to certain qualities of a project in a way that leads to understanding and appreciation. In the most successful drawings, the illustrator tells a story or sets a mood that leaves the viewer with a positive and lasting impression.

Gordon Grice, a registered architect, also pursues his interest in architectural drawing using his other voice: that of an editor. In addition to this book and several others on the subject of architectural illustration, Grice is editor of *Perspectives,* the quarterly journal of the Ontario Association of Architects.

ABOVE
PROJECT
Confederation Square
Ottawa, Ontario, Canada
CLIENT
National Capital Commission
PLANNERS
du Toit Allsopp Hillier
Toronto, Ontario, Canada
RENDERING SIZE
20" x 30" (51 cm x 76 cm)
MEDIA
Ink and pencil crayon on Mylar film

LEFT
PROJECT
Dreamland
Cairo, Egypt
CLIENT
Forrec Ltd.
Toronto, Ontario, Canada
RENDERING SIZE
20" x 30" (51 cm x 76 cm)
MEDIA
Ink and pencil crayon on Mylar film

PROJECT
Thekwini Adventure World
Durban, South Africa

CLIENT
Forrec Ltd.
Toronto, Ontario, Canada

RENDERING SIZE
18" x 32" (46 cm x 81 cm)

MEDIUM
Ink and pencil crayon on Mylar film

BELOW RIGHT
PROJECT
Alterations and Additions to an Urban Existence

RENDERING SIZE
11" x 11" (28 cm x 28 cm)

MEDIUM
Ink on bond paper

This drawing indicates how Mr. Grice would really like to live. He is a downtown person. He likes the countryside but not the location. In this wistful proposal, he suggests a solution to having it both ways. This drawing was done for a charity auction. (Reproduced with permission of Harvey Wolfe.)

77

PROJECT
Prince's Gate
Canadian National Exhibition Grounds

CLIENT
Berridge Lewinberg Greenberg Dark Gabor
Toronto, Ontario, Canada

RENDERING SIZE
20" x 20" (51 cm x 51 cm)

MEDIA
Ink and pencil crayon on Mylar film

Completed in 1993, this is a planning study for a commercial development adjacent to a venerable landmark.

The Canadian Opera Company commissioned this drawing to accompany the announcement of a design competition for a new facility. An image was required, but the building had not been designed. The illustration is a pastiche of opera references including four composers, a famous aria, the opening of a famous opera house, and a brooding Wagnerian sky with a rainbow bridge to Valhalla. For the building, the client and illustrator concocted a sort of semi-classical form and concentrated on pomp and distraction. General Manager Elaine Calder served as art director on this project.

RENDERING SIZE
8" x 10" (20 cm x 25 cm)

MEDIUM
Ink on trace

A preliminary design showing one of three proposed structures sketched over a rough computer-generated model.

RENDERING SIZE
9" x 12" (23 cm x 30 cm)

MEDIUM
Ink on trace

This first compositional sketch shows the selected building form presented in a more highly developed context.

RENDERING SIZE
9" x 12" (23 cm x 30 cm)

MEDIUM
Ink on trace

In this second compositional sketch, the viewpoint is moved to improve the drawing composition, and the computer model is developed and improved.

RIGHT
Entourage studies. The image of Gioacchino Rossini appears in the drawing shaking hands with Richard Wagner. Giuseppe Verdi is rushing by in the foreground, while Jules Massenet examines a statue in the background.

RENDERING SIZE
20" x 30" (51 cm x 76 cm)

MEDIUM
Ink on Mylar

The computer model is corrected and developed to include as much detail as possible, and a finished, full-size pencil overlay is prepared, including all entourage. After the pencil line drawing, with its tone study overlay, is approved by the client, this ink drawing is prepared.

RENDERING SIZE
20" x 30" (51 cm x 76 cm)

MEDIA
Ink and pencil crayon on Mylar film; computer-generated model

The ink line drawing is copied photographically onto specially prepared Mylar film and colored using pencil crayons from a wide variety of manufacturers, principally Derwent, to produce this final drawing.

PROJECT
Exel Insurance Head Office
Hamilton, Bermuda
ARCHITECT
Entasis
Hamilton, Bermuda
RENDERING SIZE
8" x 10" (20 cm x 25 cm)
MEDIUM
Pencil crayon on trace

These three sketches show a progression up Bermudiana Road toward the building entry, at an early design stage.

PROJECT
Savannah Centre
Lady Lake, Florida

ARCHITECT
Forrec Ltd.

RENDERING SIZE
17" x 31" (40 cm x 79 cm)

MEDIA
Ink and pencil crayon on Mylar film

CHRISTOPHER GRUBBS

CHRISTOPHER GRUBBS ILLUSTRATOR   601 4TH STREET, LOFT #112   SAN FRANCISCO, CALIFORNIA 94107   415-243-4394 TEL   415-243-4395 FAX

Christopher Grubbs likes to draw. This has led him not only to talk about and exercise his drawing skills as a teacher but also to explore them on his own terms as an artist. Most often he draws for architects, helping to get their abstract ideas into a visual form that they and their audience can better understand.

With his architectural training, intuitive nature, and quick pencil, Christopher Grubbs works with architects in the earliest days of a project, helping through exploratory sketches to develop the design. He enjoys this collaborative effort.

TITLE
Lefty O'Doul Bridge
RENDERING SIZE
28.5" x 35" (72 cm x 89 cm)
MEDIUM
Conte crayon

PROJECT
Ikspiari
Tokyo, Japan

ARCHITECT
Paul Ma Design
Berkeley, California

RENDERING SIZE
8" x 8" (20 cm x 20 cm)

MEDIA
Prismacolor on black-and-white
Xerox reproduction

PROJECT
Anonymous
Japan

ARCHITECT
Wimberly, Allison Tong & Goo
Honolulu, Hawaii

RENDERING SIZE
10" x 5" (25 cm x 13 cm)

MEDIA
Prismacolor on black-and-white
Xerox reproduction

PROJECT
Central Waterfront Development Concept Plan
Hong Kong, China

ARCHITECT
Skidmore, Owings & Merrill Architects
San Francisco, California

RENDERING SIZE
13" x 7.5" (33 cm x 19 cm)

COMPUTER MODEL
Architech Audio-Visual Ltd.
Hong Kong, China

MEDIA
Prismacolor on black-and-white Xerox
reproduction, using computer-generated model

PROJECT
Taba Heights
Egypt

ARCHITECT
Wimberly, Allison Tong & Goo
Honolulu, Hawaii

RENDERING SIZE
5" x 10" (13 cm x 25 cm)

MEDIA
Prismacolor on black-and-white
Xerox reproduction

PROJECT
Shanghai Waterfront Redevelopment
Master Plan

ARCHITECT
Skidmore, Owings & Merrill Architects
San Francisco, California

RENDERING SIZE
10" x 5" (25 cm x 13 cm)

MEDIA
Prismacolor on black-and-white
Xerox reproduction

LEFT
PROJECT
Hanoi New Town Master Plan
Hanoi, Vietnam

ARCHITECT
Skidmore, Owings & Merrill Architects
San Francisco, California

RENDERING SIZE
7" x 5" (18 cm x 13 cm)

MEDIA
Prismacolor on black-and-white
Xerox reproduction

84

BELOW
PROJECT
Fort Baker Master Plan
Marin County, California

CLIENT
Golden Gate National Parks Association

RENDERING SIZE
12" x 5" (30 cm x 13 cm)

MEDIA
Prismacolor on black-and-white
Xerox reproduction

PROJECT
San Francisco Lesbian, Gay, Bisexual &
Transgender Community Center Competition

CLIENT
Cee/Pfau Collaborative
San Francisco, California

RENDERING SIZE
10" x 8.5" (25 cm x 22 cm)

MEDIA
Prismacolor on black-and-white
Xerox reproduction

FAR RIGHT
PROJECT
Selective Insurance 1998 President's Club
Souvenir Journal

CLIENT
Incentives to Intrigue
San Francisco, California

RENDERING SIZE
3" x 7" (8 cm x 18 cm)

MEDIA
Ink and watercolor

PROJECT
Millennium Parklands
Sydney, Australia

ARCHITECT
Peter Walker and Partners
Berkeley, California

RENDERING SIZE
10" x 5" (25 cm x 13 cm)

MEDIA
Prismacolor on black-and-white
Xerox reproduction

85

PROJECT
Palace of Indigo,
Magic World Theme Park Hotel
Dubai, United Arab Emirates

ARCHITECT
Paul Ma Design
Berkeley, California

RENDERING SIZE
9.5" x 5" (24 cm x 13 cm)

MEDIA
Prismacolor on black-and-white
Xerox reproduction

PROJECT
Crissy Field

CLIENT
Hargreaves Associates
San Francisco, California

RENDERING SIZE
14" x 5" (36 cm x 13 cm)

MEDIA
Prismacolor on black-and-white
Xerox reproduction

BELOW
PROJECT
Sydney Olympics 2000 Master Concept Design
Sydney, Australia

CLIENT
Hargreaves Associates
San Francisco, California

RENDERING SIZE
16" x 10" (41 cm x 25 cm)

MEDIA
Prismacolor on black-and-white
Xerox reproduction

TITLE
The Narrows, Tassajara Zen Mountain Center
RENDERING SIZE
11" x 14" (28 cm x 36 cm)
MEDIUM
Pencil

BELOW
TITLE
The Narrows, Tassajara Zen Mountain Center
RENDERING SIZE
9" x 12" (23 cm x 30 cm)
MEDIUM
Ink and brush

87

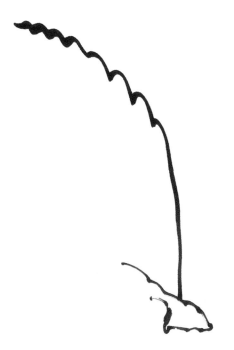

STEPHAN HOFFPAUIR, AIA

640 WALAVISTA AVENUE   OAKLAND, CALIFORNIA 94610   510-272-9794 TEL   510-272-9794 FAX

More than a decade ago, Stephan Hoffpauir was one of a handful of artists working to revive the forgotten art of watercolor architectural drawings. *Architectural Illustration in Watercolor,* a book he co-authored and illustrated, was the first of its kind to be published in decades. Since then, watercolor has been widely embraced as a medium by architectural illustrators, and Stephan Hoffpauir has become known as one of the leading figures in his field.

"Of course, I want to produce beautiful drawings, but I also want to establish a lasting, trusting relationship with a client," says Hoffpauir. "I always ask new clients how my drawings will be used and how they expect them to look when finished. If I do not pay attention to their needs in the beginning, they will not be happy in the end, no matter how beautiful the drawing." Hoffpauir's loyal and expanding client base is testament to his sense of concern.

PROJECT
Electrical Power Station
ARCHITECT
Antonio Sant'Elia
RENDERING SIZE
10.5" x 16" (27 cm x 41 cm)
MEDIUM
Watercolor

BELOW
PROJECT
Plant and Environmental Sciences Replacement Facility, University of California
Davis, California
ARCHITECT
Zimmer Gunsul Frasca Partnership
RENDERING SIZE
13" x 24" (33 cm x 61 cm)
MEDIUM
Watercolor

OPPOSITE
PROJECT
One South Market
San José, California
ARCHITECT
Skidmore, Owings & Merrill Architects
RENDERING SIZE
14" x 21" (36 cm x 53 cm)
MEDIUM
Watercolor

PROJECT
Good Samaritan Hospital
Portland, Oregon

ARCHITECT
Johnson Design Studio Architecture

RENDERING SIZE
21" x 22" (53 cm x 56 cm)

MEDIUM
Watercolor

PROJECT
Shilla Hotel, Presidential Suite
Seoul, South Korea

ARCHITECT
Babey Moulton Inc.

RENDERING SIZE
14" x 14" (36 cm x 36 cm)

MEDIUM
Watercolor

BELOW
PROJECT
Shilla Hotel, Presidential Suite
Seoul, South Korea

ARCHITECT
Babey Moulton Inc.

RENDERING SIZE
16" x 24" (41 cm x 61 cm)

MEDIUM
Watercolor

LEFT
PROJECT
Xinmin
Shanghai Evening Newspaper Building
Shanghai, China

ARCHITECT
Hellmuth, Obata + Kassabaum

RENDERING SIZE
16" x 24" (41 cm x 61 cm)

MEDIUM
Watercolor

BELOW
PROJECT
Alkent 2000
Istanbul, Turkey

ARCHITECT
Sandy & Babcock International

RENDERING SIZE
14" x 21" (36 cm x 53 cm)

MEDIUM
Watercolor

ABOVE
PROJECT
Stanford Research Park
Palo Alto, California

ARCHITECT
Korth Sunseri Hagey Architects

RENDERING SIZE
17" x 25.5" (43 cm x 65 cm)

MEDIUM
Watercolor

THIS PAGE
PROJECT
Donghia Hotel and Villa
Shanghai, China

ARCHITECT
Hellmuth, Obata + Kassabaum

RENDERING SIZE
18" x 27" (46 cm x 69 cm)

MEDIUM
Watercolor

92

PROFESSIONAL AFFILIATIONS
American Institute of Architects
American Society of Architectural Perspectivists
San Francisco Society of Illustrators

PROJECT
Sony Station Virtual Theme Park

DESIGNERS
CKS Partners
Stephan Hoffpauir

RENDERING SIZE
16" x 24" (41 cm x 61 cm)

MEDIUM
Watercolor

BELOW
PROJECT
Contained Research Facility
University of California
Davis, California

ARCHITECT
Anshen + Allen

RENDERING SIZE
18" x 27" (46 cm x 69 cm)

MEDIUM
Watercolor

LEFT
PROJECT
Contained Research Facility
University of California
Davis, California

ARCHITECT
Anshen + Allen

RENDERING SIZE
18" x 27" (46 cm x 69 cm)

MEDIUM
Watercolor

CLIENT LIST

Anshen + Allen

Asian Art Museum of San Francisco

Brøderbund Software

CKS Partners

Film Institute of Northern California

Gensler and Associates

Hellmuth, Obata + Kassabaum

Kaplan McLaughlin Diaz

Kohn Pedersen Fox Conway

Landor Associates

SOM

Sasaki Associates, Inc.

Sony Technologies

Stanford University

University of California

Zimmer Gunsul Frasca Partnership

WILLIAM HOOK

W.G. HOOK ARCHITECTURAL ILLUSTRATION   1501 WESTERN AVE., SUITE 500   SEATTLE, WASHINGTON 98101   206-622-3849 TEL   206-624-1494 FAX

Bill Hook started a second career in architectural illustration after fifteen years as an architect. Now, almost fifteen years later, he is still enjoying the challenge of creating visions of the future, always pursuing the potential of the pencil and transparent watercolor to capture the illusive qualities of light and atmosphere needed to bring life and a sense of time and place to the plans of designers and developers.

His extensive architectural experience gives him not only an intimate understanding of the creative design process and the ability to translate ideas into an accessible visual form, but also an understanding of the critical role quality illustrations play in assuring the success of a project. Working as an illustrator has furthered his understanding of and insight into the importance of site and context. He also possesses a profound respect for the long-term vision provided by landscape architects and planners. Bill Hook often approaches a set of drawings as a photographer approaches an assignment—by "walking around"—the project to discover the most appropriate, rather than the most obvious, views to convey the intent of the drawing and spirit of the design.

ABOVE
PROJECT
Freestone Lodge
Mazama, Washington
ARCHITECT
Leavengood Architects
Seattle, Washington
RENDERING SIZE
15" x 30" (38 cm x 76 cm)
MEDIUM
Watercolor

BELOW
PROJECT
Osprey Lodge
Jackson, Wyoming
ARCHITECT
Leavengood Architects
Seattle, Washington
RENDERING SIZE
8" x 20" (20 cm x 51 cm)
MEDIUM
Pencil

OPPOSITE
PROJECT
Swedish Medical Center
Seattle, Washington
ARCHITECT
NBBJ
Seattle, Washington
RENDERING SIZE
35" x 22" (89 cm x 56 c
MEDIUM
Watercolor

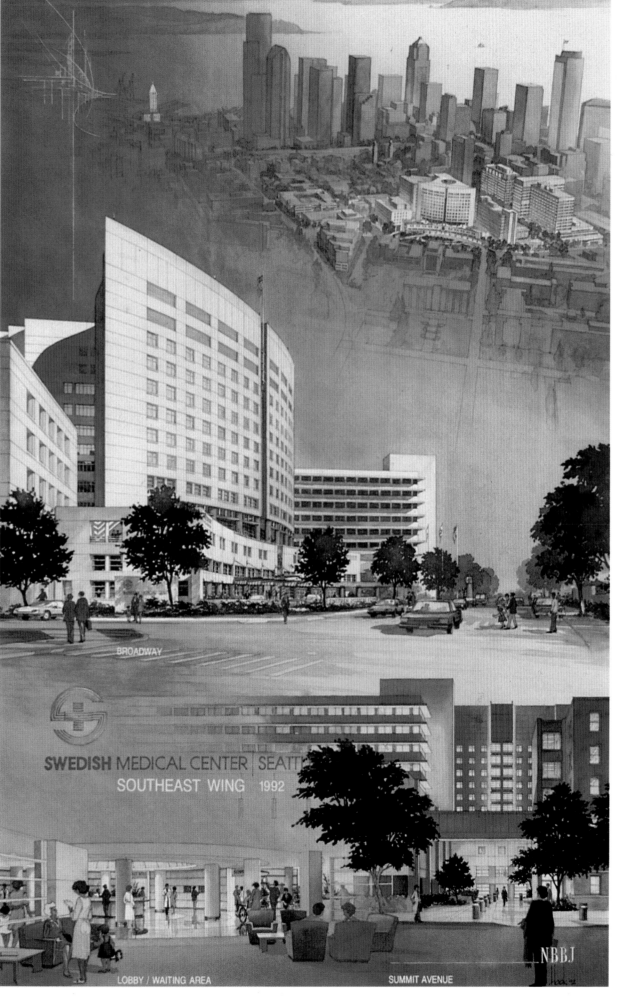

BROADWAY

SWEDISH MEDICAL CENTER | SEATTLE
SOUTHEAST WING 1992

LOBBY / WAITING AREA

SUMMIT AVENUE

NBBJ

PROJECT
East Capitol Campus, Plan
Washington State Capitol
Olympia, Washington
ARCHITECT
EDAW
Seattle, Washington
MEDIUM
Watercolor

BELOW
PROJECT
Great Hall,
St. Mary's College
St. Mary's City, Maryland
ARCHITECT
Hartman Cox Architects
Washington, DC
RENDERING SIZE
11" x 17" (28 cm x 43 cm)
MEDIUM
Pencil

BELOW
PROJECT
St. Mary's College
St. Mary's City, Maryland
ARCHITECT
Hartman Cox Architects
Washington, DC
RENDERING SIZE
13" x 22" (33 cm x 56 cm)
MEDIUM
Watercolor

PROJECT
Hall of Still Thoughts
Tzu Chi Foundation
Tai Ching, Taiwan

ARCHITECT
NBBJ
Seattle, Washington

RENDERING SIZE
17" x 11" (43 cm x 28 cm)

MEDIUM
Pencil

This is a conceptual design feedback
sketch. Sketch Category Award,
Architecture in Perspective 14.

BELOW
PROJECT
Samsung Global Gateway Project
Changwon, South Korea

ARCHITECT
NBBJ
Seattle, Washington

RENDERING SIZE
14" x 11" (36 cm x 28 cm)

MEDIUM
Watercolor

BELOW
PROJECT
Benaroya Hall, Seattle Symphony
Seattle, Washington

ARCHITECT
LMN Architects
Seattle, Washington

RENDERING SIZE
13" x 22" (33 cm x 56 cm)

MEDIUM
Watercolor

PROJECT
Reebok World Headquarters
Canton, Massachusetts

ARCHITECT
NBBJ
Seattle, Washington

RENDERING SIZE
16" x 30" (41 cm x 776 cm)

MEDIUM
Pencil
This is a concept sketch of the lobby.

LEFT
PROJECT
Georgetown Waterfront
Alexandria, Virginia

ARCHITECT
EDAW
Alexandria, Virginia

RENDERING SIZE
5" x 8.5" (13 cm x 22 cm)

MEDIUM
Watercolor

BELOW
PROJECT
Hec Edmundson Pavilion
University of Washington
Seattle, Washington

ARCHITECT
LMN Architects
Seattle, Washington

RENDERING SIZE
13" x 24" (33 cm x 61 cm)

MEDIUM
Watercolor

PROJECT
Mariners Ballpark Proposal
Seattle, Washington
ARCHITECT
NBBJ
Seattle, Washington
RENDERING SIZE
12" x 20" (30 cm x 51 cm)
MEDIUM
Watercolor (detail)

BELOW
PROJECT
Reebok World Headquarters
Canton, Massachusetts
ARCHITECT
NBBJ
Seattle, Washington
RENDERING SIZE
17" x 28" (43 cm x 71 cm)
MEDIUM
Watercolor

PARTIAL CLIENT LIST
NBBJ, Seattle, San Francisco, Los Angeles
LMN Architects, Seattle, Washington
Hartman Cox Architects, Washington, DC
Zimmer Gunsul Frasca Partnership, Seattle, Washington
Leavengood Architects, Seattle, Washington
Stephen Sullivan Architects, Seattle, Washington
The Rockwell Group, New York, New York
EDAW, Alexandria, Seattle, San Francisco
Mitchell Matthews & Associates, Charlottesville, Virginia
James Cutler Architects, Bainbridge Island, Washington
Miller Hull, Seattle, Washington
Gordon Walker Architect, Seattle, Washington
Wimberly, Allison, Tong & Goo, Honolulu, Hawaii
Reebok, Canton, Massachusetts
Seattle Symphony, Seattle, Washington
Walt Disney Imagineering, Anaheim, California
Chihuly Studio, Seattle, Washington
Elkus Manfredi Architects, Ltd., Boston, Massachusetts
National Academy of Sciences, Washington, D.C.

PROFESSIONAL AFFILIATIONS
President Emeritus, Advisory Council, American Society
of Architectural Perspectivists

PUBLICATIONS
Architecture In Watercolor, Thomas Schaller
The Wright Space, Grant Hildebrand
Streetcar Suburb, Casey Rosenberg
Architecture in Perspective Exhibits 2, 3, 5, 6, 8, 9, 12
Architectural Rendering, Phillip Crowe
NBBJ—The Master Architect Series II

99

AWARDS
Sketch Category, Architecture in Perspective 14
Award of Excellence, Architecture in Perspective 2, 3, 5,
6, 8, 9, 12

HOWARD HUIZING

145 SOUTH OLIVE STREET   ORANGE, CALIFORNIA 92866   714-532-3012 TEL   714-532-5298 FAX

It is a continuing marvel that a simple line on a page or the delicate nuance of a watercolor wash can be crafted to communicate a wealth of information and to provide a visual experience of delight. Howard Huizing enjoys providing illustrations that inform the mind while captivating the imagination. A boyhood love of architecture has developed into a professional practice of over thirty years of designing, teaching, and illustrating within the architectural community.

In our fast-paced professional world, with its rapidly advancing technological opportunities, the human demand for architectural (and by association, illustrative) excellence remains a constant. Huizing, by providing a variety of techniques and media, is able to customize an image to a project's unique requirement. His goal is to create each image in a manner that not only illustrates and informs, but also intrigues and delights. Architecture as drawn on a page can be a graphic portrayal of great power even as it entices the eye to accept that which is imagined as that which is believable.

ABOVE
PROJECT
McCartney Library, Geneva College
Beaver Falls, Pennsylvania
RENDERING SIZE
8" x 5" (20 cm x 13 cm)
MEDIUM
Ink line drawing

LEFT
PROJECT
Corona Factory Stores
Corona, California
ARCHITECT
Architects Orange
Orange, California
RENDERING SIZE
16" x 20" (41 cm x 51 cm)
MEDIUM
Ink line drawing

PROJECT
Fullerton Arboretum
Fullerton, California

ARCHITECT
Tom Lennon
Fullerton, California

RENDERING SIZE
17" x 27" (43 cm x 69 cm)

MEDIUM
Ink line drawing

RIGHT
PROJECT
South Fair Oaks
Redevelopment Plan
Pasadena, California

ARCHITECT
Marc A. Futterman and Associates
Los Angeles, California

RENDERING SIZE
10" x 13" (25 cm x 33 cm)

MEDIA
Ink line and watercolor

PROJECT
Pickfair
Beverly Hills, California

ARCHITECT
Wallace Neff, FAIA

RENDERING SIZE
20" x 28" (51 cm x 71 cm)

MEDIUM
Transparent watercolor

This illustration was created from archival images; the structure has been demolished.

LEFT
PROJECT
Air Traffic Control Tower
Port Columbus Airport
Columbus, Ohio

ARCHITECT
Holmes and Narver, Inc.
Orange, California

RENDERING SIZE
25" x 20" (64 cm x 51 cm)

MEDIA
Ink line and watercolor

BELOW
PROJECT
Culver House
Cheviot Hills, California

ARCHITECT
Wallace Neff, FAIA

RENDERING SIZE
17" x 28" (43 cm x 71 cm)

MEDIUM
Transparent watercolor

As the structure has been demolished, this illustration was created from archival images.

PROJECT
Private Residence
Beijing, China
ARCHITECT
McClellan/Cruz/Gaylord & Associates
Pasadena, California
RENDERING SIZE
10" x 13" (25 cm x 33 cm)
MEDIUM
Colored pencil

PROJECT
Memorial Hall, Chapman University
Orange, California
RENDERING SIZE
9" x 13" (23 cm x 33 cm)
MEDIA
Ink line and watercolor

PROJECT
Williamsburg Courthouse Competition
Williamsburg, Virginia
ARCHITECT
Parallax Associates, Inc.
Beverly Hills, California
RENDERING SIZE
10" x 14" (25 cm x 36 cm)
MEDIUM
Colored pencil

PROJECT
St. Anthony's Parish
Phoenix, Arizona

ARCHITECT
Bissell Architects
Newport Beach, California

RENDERING SIZE
18" x 12" (46 cm x 30 cm)

MEDIUM
Colored pencil

PROJECT
Private Residence
Newport Beach, California

ARCHITECTS
Ade Collie Architect
Orange, California
and EBTA/Architects
Irvine, California

RENDERING SIZE
13.5" x 20" (33 cm x 51 cm)

MEDIUM
Transparent watercolor

LEFT
PROJECT
Ritter Ranch
Palmdale, California

ARCHITECT
The KTGY Group
Irvine, California

RENDERING SIZE
13" x 15" (33 cm x 38 cm)

MEDIA
Colored pencil

BELOW
PROJECT
Rio Piedras Station
San Juan, Puerto Rico

ARCHITECT
Sverdrup Civil, Inc.
Costa Mesa, California

RENDERING SIZE
24" x 34" (61 cm x 86 cm)

MEDIA
Ink line and colored pencil

PROJECT
Liberty Development Communities
Lake Elsinore, California

ARCHITECT
Cooper Robertson & Partners
New York, New York
Scheurer Architects, Inc.
Newport Beach, California

RENDERING SIZE
8" x 12" (20 cm x 30 cm)

MEDIUM
Ink line drawing

RIGHT
PROJECT
Liberty Development Communities
Lake Elsinore, California

ARCHITECT
Cooper Robertson & Partners
New York, New York
Scheurer Architects, Inc.
Newport Beach, California

RENDERING SIZE
8" x 12" (20 cm x 30 cm)

MEDIUM
Ink line drawing

PROFESSIONAL AFFILIATIONS

American Society of Architectural Perspectivists

DOUGLAS E. JAMIESON

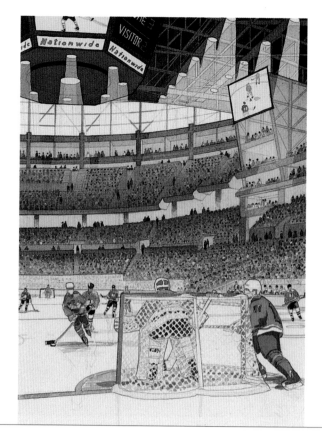

827 VIA DE LA PAZ   PACIFIC PALISADES, CALIFORNIA 90272   310-573-1155 TEL   310-573-1685 FAX

Doug Jamieson is a professional illustrator based in Los Angeles, where he has practiced for more than a decade. His practice has evolved and expanded to accommodate the varying demands of today's profession, utilizing not only his experience as a Hugh Ferriss Award-winning illustrator but also his talents as a designer and architect. This combination of skills proves invaluable to clients whose design ideas have yet to be fully realized.

Light, color, and composition are the exceptional qualities displayed in Jamieson's work, as well as a strong sense of atmosphere, a timeless sense of style, and a great abstract finesse.

THIS PAGE
PROJECT
Nationwide Arena,
NHL Expansion Columbus Bluejackets
Columbus, Ohio
ARCHITECT
NBBJ
MEDIA
Watercolor over pencil

OPPOSITE
PROJECT
Desert Passage at Aladdin Casino
Las Vegas, Nevada
ARCHITECT
Trizec Hahn Development Corporation
San Diego, California
MEDIA
Watercolor over pencil

PROJECT
Menara Bakrie Tower
Jakarta, Indonesia

ARCHITECT
DMJM Keating
Los Angeles, California

MEDIA
Watercolor over pencil

OPPOSITE

PROJECT
Opus Office Tower
Los Angeles, California

ARCHITECT
Opus Development
Los Angeles, California

MEDIA
Watercolor over pencil

PROJECT
Royce Hall Renovation
University of California
Los Angeles, California

MEDIUM
Watercolor over pencil

PROJECT
610 Park Avenue
New York, New York

ARCHITECT
Colony Advisors

MEDIA
Watercolor over pencil

LEFT
PROJECT
United States Embassy
Berlin, Germany

ARCHITECT
Moore Ruble Yudell
Los Angeles, California

MEDIA
Watercolor over pencil

PROJECT
Kaiser Hospital
Oakland, California

ARCHITECT
Kaplan McLaughlin Diaz

MEDIA
Watercolor over pencil

CLIENT LIST

Anchen + Allen, Los Angeles, San Francisco, California

Arquitectura, Miami, Florida

Catellus Development, Los Angeles, San Francisco, California

DMJM Keating, Los Angeles, California

Dworsky Associates, Los Angeles, California

Gensler and Associates, Los Angeles, California

The Getty Museum, Los Angeles, California

Gruen Associates, Los Angeles, California

Hellmuth, Obata + Kassabaum, Los Angeles, San Francisco,
California; Hong Kong, China

Kaplan McLaughlin Diaz, San Francisco, California

Maguire Thomas Partners, Los Angeles, California

Michael Wilford and Associates, London, England

Moore Ruble Yudell, Los Angeles, California

Moshe Safdie and Associates, Boston, Massachusetts

NGGJ, Los Angeles, California; Seattle, Washington; Columbus, Ohio

Nikken Sekkei International, Singapore

Opus Development, Los Angeles, California

Pei, Cobb, Freed & Partners, New York, New York

Rockwellgroup, New York

RTKL Associates, Los Angeles

Skidmore, Owings, and Merrill Architects,
Los Angeles, San Francisco, , California; New York, New York

Trizechahn, San Diego, California

University of California, Los Angeles, California

Walt Disney Imagineering, Los Angeles, California

Zeidler Roberts Partnership, Toronto, Ontario, Canada;
London, England

AWARDS

The Hugh Ferriss Memorial Prize

Jurors Awards

Jean Paul Carlhian Award 1990

Ronald Love Award 1994

Award of Distinction

Honor Awards

Architecture in Perspective 5, 6, 7, 8, 9, 10;
1990–1995

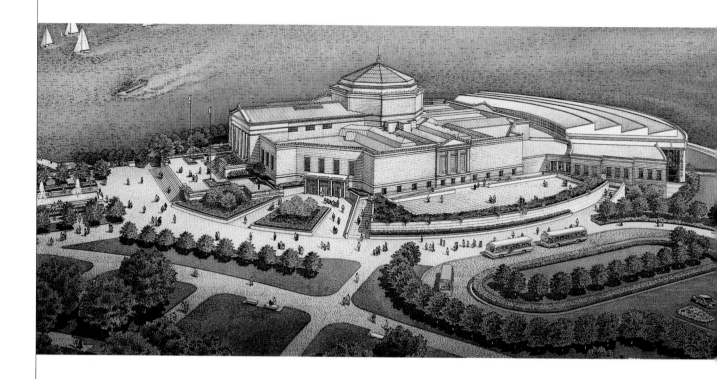

YOUNG H. KI

YOUNG H. KI & ASSOCIATES 8 SOUTH MICHIGAN AVENUE, SUITE 310 CHICAGO, ILLINOIS 60603 312-332-2422 TEL 312-332-2482 FAX
YHKA@WORLDNET.ATT.NET

Young H. Ki is an architect and architectural artist whose work transcends the limited purposes for which it is produced and merits independent consideration as fine art. With more than twenty-three years of experience, Young Ki works as an architect with Skidmore, Owings & Merrill in Chicago and serves as key renderer and vice president of Rael D. Slutsky & Associates. He is also a member of both the Korean Institute of Architect (KIA) and the American Society of Architectural Perspectivists (ASAP) and currently serves as ASAP's International Coordinator. His work has been displayed in several exhibits and has been featured in numerous major publications. With his extensive architectural background, Young Ki has a thorough understanding of the 3-D environment. The dramatic and detailed style of his pen-and-ink renderings yields vividly realistic images.

ABOVE
PROJECT
The John G. Shedd Aquarium
Chicago, Illinois
ARCHITECT
Ross Barney + Jankowski, Architects
Chicago, Illinois
MEDIA
Pen and ink with watercolor
This illustration shows the addition of Phillipines Exhibition.

PROJECT
Kimhae Cultural Center
Kimhae, South Korea

ARCHITECTS
The Leonard Parker Associates
Minneapolis, Minnesota
Sammin Architects
Seoul, South Korea

MEDIA
Pen and ink with watercolor and airbrush

This illustration was part of an international design competition entry.

ABOVE RIGHT
PROJECT
Jaeju Cultural Center
Jaeju, Korea

ARCHITECT
Ki C. Bae + Arakaya

MEDIA
Pen and ink with watercolor

This illustration was a design competition entry.

Young H. Ki and his associates' initial study of a project involves scrupulous planning: The "simple" step of selecting a view requires exact calculation, careful study, and precise measurement—not to mention a great deal of imagination. In his studio, Ki maintains a complete library of architectural materials, including lighting effects, color studies, and landscaping information, for reference when creating his images.

CLIENT LIST

Anderson & Oh, Chicago, Illinois

Cesar Pelli & Associates, New Haven, Connecticut

Daniel P. Coffey & Associates, Chicago, Illinois

DeStefano Partners, Chicago, Illinois

Dongbu Engineering, Seoul, South Korea

Gruen Associates, Los Angeles, California

Harry Wees Associates, Chicago, Illinois

Hellmuth, Obata + Kassabaum, Tampa, Florida; St. Louis, Missouri; Washington, D.C.

Holabrid & Root, Chicago, Illinois

Kunwon International, Seoul, South Korea

Murphy/Jahn Architects, Chicago, Illinois

Namsan Architects, Seoul, South Korea

Perkins & Will, Chicago, Illinois

Philip Johnson, New York, New York

Phillips Swager Associates, Naperville Illinois

RTKL Associates, Baltimore, Maryland

Samwoo Architects, Seoul, South Korea

Space Group of Korea, Seoul, South Korea

Skidmore, Owings & Merrill, San Francisco, California

Tai Soo Kim Partners, Hartford, Connecticut

The Leonard Parker Associates, Minneapolis, Minnesota

Urban Design Group, Northbrook, Illinois

OPPOSITE
PROJECT
The National Museum of Korea
Seoul, South Korea

ARCHITECTS
Anderson & Oh
Chicago, Illinois
Phillip Johnson
New York, New York

MEDIA
Mixed computer-generated and hand-drawn pen and ink with colored pencil and pastel

This illustration was an International Design Competition entry.

PROJECT
New Schaumburg Township District Library

ARCHITECT
Phillips Swager Associates

MEDIA
Pen and ink with colored pencil and pastel

This illustration features both daytime and nighttime views of the library.

PROJECT
Yecheon Community College
Yecheon, South Korea

ARCHITECTS
Anderson & Oh
Chicago, Illinois
Studio ASOC

MEDIA
Pen and ink with watercolor and colored pencil

This illustration was part of a design competition entry.

ABOVE LEFT
PROJECT
The National Police Academy
Yongin, South Korea

ARCHITECTS
Anderson & Oh
Chicago, Illinois
Garim Architects
Seoul, South Korea

MEDIA
Pen and ink with watercolor

This illustration was part of a design competition entry.

BELOW
PROJECT
The Training Academy of KNSPB
South Korea

ARCHITECT
Anderson & Oh

MEDIA
Pen and ink with colored pencil and pastel

These illustrations were part of a design competition entry.

BELOW RIGHT
PROJECT
Inchon Science Academy
Inchon, South Korea

ARCHITECTS
BSK Design Studio
Tae Architects & Engineers Group

MEDIA
Pen and ink with watercolor

LEFT
PROJECT
West Connecticut University Dormitory

ARCHITECT
Tai Soo Kim Partners
Hartford, Connecticut

MEDIA
Formal pen and ink with colored pencil and pastel

This illustration was part of a design competition entry.

PROJECT
Kwangiu City Hall
Kwangiu, Korea

ARCHITECTS
Young H. Ki & Associates
Embiance, UG

MEDIA
Mixed computer-generated and hand-drawn
pen and ink with watercolor

This illustration was part of a design
competition entry.

PROJECT
The New District Prosecutor's
Office Building
Inchon, South Korea

ARCHITECTS
Anderson & Oh
Tae Architects

MEDIA
Pen and ink with watercolor and airbrush

This illustration was part of a design
competition entry.

BELOW
PROJECT
Jinjiu City Hall
Jinjiu, Korea

ARCHITECT
Namsan Architects

MEDIA
Pen and ink with watercolor and airbrush

This illustration was part of a design
competition entry.

PROJECT
Riverbend
Chicago, Illinois

ARCHITECT
DeStefano and Partners Ltd.

MEDIA
Mixed computer-generated and hand-drawn
pen and ink with watercolor and airbrush

RIGHT
PROJECT
Hanjoong Industries and Information Center
Seoul, South Korea

ARCHITECTS
Anderson & Oh
Haenglim Architects

MEDIA
Formal pen and ink with colored pencil and pastel

This illustration was part of a design
competition entry.

PROJECT
Kyungju High Speed Railway Station
Kyungju, Korea

ARCHITECTS
Anderson & Oh
Harry Wees Associates

MEDIA
Mixed computer-generated and hand-drawn
pen and ink with watercolor and airbrush

This illustration was part of a design
competition entry.

ABOVE AND ABOVE RIGHT
PROJECT
Korean Agricultural and Aquatic Trade
Promotion Center
Seoul, South Korea

ARCHITECTS
Perkins & Will
Chicago, Illinois
Mooyoung Architect

MEDIA
Pen and ink with colored pencil and pastel
(daytime view); pen and ink with watercolor
and airbrush (nighttime view)

RIGHT AND BELOW
PROJECT
Alpha Hotel and Marina
Beirut, Lebanon

ARCHITECT
Perkins & Will
Chicago, Illinois

MEDIA
Pen and ink with colored pencil and pastel

This illustration shows an aerial view rendering
and a marina close-up view rendering.

SUN-HO LEE

EHO DESIGN SUK JUN BUILDING, #601 364-31 SEOGYO-DONG MAPO-GU   SEOUL 121-210 KOREA 82-2-334-2118 EXT. 7090 TEL 82-2-338-9416 FAX

EHO Design was established in 1979 with Sun-Ho Lee as the president. In the beginning, the firm focused on architectural illustration; as of 1985 however, EHO Design expanded to include the creation of architectural models. In the past three decades, construction of modern buildings in South Korea has been on the rise. Paralleling this growth, Lee's firm has undertaken many exciting projects.

EHO Design has the ability to provide both illustration and modeling services. Recently, the firm has developed into a total design company, handling both interior design and exhibition design projects. Still, Sun-Ho Lee's passion lies in the artistic rendering of architectural illustration.

ABOVE
PROJECT
Posco Building
Seoul, South Korea

ARCHITECT
Kan Sam Architects, Ltd.
Seoul, South Korea

RENDERING SIZE
23.375" x 37" (59 cm x 94 cm)

MEDIUM
Gouache

LEFT
PROJECT
Passenger Terminal and Surrounding Area
Inchon, South Korea

ARCHITECT
Aum & Lee Architects, Ltd.
Seoul, South Korea

RENDERING SIZE
23.375" x 33" (59 cm x 84 cm)

MEDIUM
Gouache

PROJECT
Roward for High Speed Electronic
Railway Terminal
Pusan, South Korea

ARCHITECT
Jung Lim Architects, Ltd.
Seoul, South Korea

RENDERING SIZE
33" x 11.375" (84 cm x 12 cm)

MEDIUM
Airbrush on black board

RIGHT
PROJECT
Shin Dong A Life Building
Seoul, South Korea

ARCHITECT
Jung Lim Architects, Ltd.
Seoul, South Korea

RENDERING SIZE
23.375" x 33" (59 cm x 84 cm)

MEDIUM
Gouache

PROJECT
Vision City
Kuala Lumpur, Malaysia

ARCHITECT
Space Group Architects, Ltd.
Seoul, South Korea

RENDERING SIZE
39.375" x 23.5" (40 cm x 60 cm)

MEDIUM
Airbrush

RIGHT
PROJECT
Chung Chong Bank
Daejon, South Korea

ARCHITECT
Jung Lim Architects, Ltd.
Seoul, South Korea

RENDERING SIZE
23.375" x 33" (59 cm x 84 cm)

MEDIUM
Watercolor

LEFT
PROJECT
Asian and West Architecture in Duksu Palace
RENDERING SIZE
14.25" x 10.625" (36.5 cm x 26.5 cm)
MEDIUM
Watercolor

BELOW
PROJECT
Korean Traditional Royal Palace Wall
Duksu Palace
RENDERING SIZE
12.5" x 10" (32 cm x 25 cm)
MEDIUM
Watercolor

PROJECT
Yudo Bank Town Construction
Seoul, South Korea
RENDERING SIZE
19.5" x 27.5" (50 cm x 70 cm)
MEDIUM
Pen

RENDERING SIZE
26.875" x 17.5" (68 cm x 44 cm)
MEDIUM
Watercolor

PROJECT
Korea Communication Company Building
Seoul, South Korea

ARCHITECT
Kum Sung Architects, Ltd.
Seoul, South Korea

RENDERING SIZE
23.375" x 33" (59 cm x 84 cm)

MEDIA
Pen and ink with watercolor

LEFT
PROJECT
Kwangju Bank Building

ARCHITECT
Space Group Architects, Ltd.
Seoul, South Korea

RENDERING SIZE
23.375" x 33" (59 cm x 84 cm)

MEDIUM
Gouache

PROJECT
Travel Expo
Sokcho, South Korea

ARCHITECT
Min Kyung Sik Architects, Ltd.
Seoul, South Korea

RENDERING SIZE
23.375" x 33" (59 cm x 84 cm)

MEDIUM
Airbrush

PROJECT
Tongil Chonmang Dae

ARCHITECT
Jinwon Architects, Ltd.
Seoul, South Korea

RENDERING SIZE
19.5" x 27.5" (50 cm x 70 cm)

MEDIUM
Gouache

At this place, one can see North Korea from South
Korea; beyond the river is North Korea.

PROJECT
Chunhai Nursery College
Ulsan, South Korea

ARCHITECT
Cho Byung Su Architects, Ltd.
Seoul, South Korea

RENDERING SIZE
15.875" x 23.5" (40 cm x 60 cm)

MEDIA
Watercolor and airbrush

RIGHT
RENDERING SIZE
13.875" x 15.875" (35 cm x 40 cm)

MEDIUM
Watercolor

RENDERING SIZE
15.875" x 17.875" (40 cm x 45 cm)

MEDIUM
Watercolor

BELOW
PROJECT
Hyundai Haisang Building
Seoul, South Korea

ARCHITECT
Jung Lim Architects, Ltd.
Seoul, South Korea

RENDERING SIZE
23.375" x 33" (59 cm x 84 cm)

MEDIA
Pen and ink with watercolor

PROJECT
Reward for Korea Industry Bank
Seoul, South Korea

ARCHITECT
Jung Lim Architects, Ltd.
Seoul, South Korea

RENDERING SIZE
23.375" x 33" (59 cm x 84 cm)

MEDIUM
Gouache

RIGHT
RENDERING SIZE
6.5" x 15" (17 cm x 38 cm)

MEDIUM
Watercolor

BELOW
PROJECT
Korea Electronic Power Company Building
Seoul, South Korea

ARCHITECT
G. O. Architects, Ltd.
Seoul, South Korea

RENDERING SIZE
15.875" x 23.5" (40 cm x 60 cm)

MEDIUM
Watercolor

LAURA CLAYTON LINN

HELLMUTH, OBATA + KASSABAUM   ONE METROPOLITAN SQUARE   211 NORTH BROADWAY, SUITE 600   ST. LOUIS, MISSOURI 63102
314-421-2000 TEL   314-421-6073 FAX

Laura Clayton Linn leads the in-house illustration department at the world-renowned architectural firm of Hellmuth, Obata + Kassabaum. Having been with the firm since 1993, she serves illustration and presentation needs throughout the firm including various groups within HOK such as planning, interiors, marketing, science and technology, justice, health care, and entertainment. Linn combines her love for watercolor with her natural ability for perspective drawing, resulting in high-detail renderings, which are tailored to the needs of each presentation.

Laura Linn's artwork has been displayed in worldwide exhibitions and publications associated with the American Society of Architectural Perspectivists, "Architectural illustration is a wonderful career for me because it's the perfect combination of the elements that make up my educational background: artistic creativity with more technical architecture and design."

ABOVE
PROJECT
BJC Hospital
South Campus Integration Project
St. Louis, Missouri

ARCHITECT
Hellmuth, Obata + Kassabaum
St. Louis, Missouri

RENDERING SIZE
14.5" x 10.5" (37 cm x 27 cm)

MEDIUM
Watercolor

LEFT
PROJECT
BJC Hospital
North Campus Integration Project
St. Louis, Missouri

ARCHITECT
Hellmuth, Obata + Kassabaum
St. Louis, Missouri

RENDERING SIZE
14.5" x 10.5" (37 cm x 27 cm)

MEDIUM
Watercolor

PROJECT
BJC
Campus Integration Project
St. Louis, Missouri

ARCHITECT
Hellmuth, Obata + Kassabaum
St. Louis, Missouri

RENDERING SIZE
15.5" x 10" (39 cm x 25 cm)

MEDIUM
Watercolor

This illustration shows an aerial view of the project.

PROJECT
Missouri Historical Society Museum
New Addition
St. Louis, Missouri

ARCHITECT
Hellmuth, Obata + Kassabaum
St. Louis, Missouri

RENDERING SIZE
19.5" x 18.5" (50 cm x 47 cm)

MEDIUM
Watercolor

ABOVE RIGHT
PROJECT
Northern Kentucky University
New Science Building
Covington, Kentucky

ARCHITECT
Hellmuth, Obata + Kassabaum
St. Louis, Missouri

RENDERING SIZE
18.5" x 12" (47 cm x 30 cm)

MEDIUM
Watercolor

RIGHT
PROJECT
Scrushy Building, University of Alabama
Birmingham, Alabama

ARCHITECT
Hellmuth, Obata + Kassabaum
St. Louis, Missouri

RENDERING SIZE
13.5" x 14.5" (34 cm x 37 cm)

MEDIUM
Watercolor

LEFT

PROJECT
University of Missouri, New Chemistry Building
Columbia, Missouri

ARCHITECT
Hellmuth, Obata + Kassabaum
St. Louis, Missouri

RENDERING SIZE
16.5" x 9" (42 cm x 23 cm)

MEDIUM
Watercolor

PROJECT
Harrington Museum, Southern Illinois University
Edwardsville, Illinois

ARCHITECT
Hellmuth, Obata + Kassabaum
St. Louis, Missouri

RENDERING SIZE
15.5" x 9.5" (39 cm x 24 cm)

MEDIUM
Watercolor

PROJECT
Denver Courthouse
Denver, Colorado

ARCHITECT
Hellmuth, Obata + Kassabaum
St. Louis, Missouri
with Anderson Mason Dale
Denver, Colorado

OWNER
General Services Administration
Denver, Colorado

RENDERING SIZE
17" x 11" (43 cm x 28 cm)

MEDIUM
Watercolor

ABOVE
PROJECT
Illinois Juvenile Corrections Center
Kewanee, Illinois

ARCHITECT
Hellmuth, Obata + Kassabaum
St. Louis, Missouri

RENDERING SIZE
24.5" x 14" (62 cm x 36 cm)

MEDIUM
Watercolor

ABOVE RIGHT
PROJECT
St. Louis City Justice Center
St. Louis, Missouri

ARCHITECT
Hellmuth, Obata + Kassabaum
St. Louis, Missouri
Kennedy Associates
St. Louis, Missouri

RENDERING SIZE
14.5" x 10.5" (37 cm x 27 cm)

MEDIUM
Watercolor

RIGHT
PROJECT
Gateway Museum
East St. Louis, Illinois

ARCHITECT
Gyo Obata and Elysse Newman of
Hellmuth, Obata + Kassabaum
St. Louis, Missouri

RENDERING SIZE
10" x 10" (25 cm x 25 cm)

MEDIUM
Watercolor

PROJECT
Boeing Learning Center
St. Louis, Missouri

ARCHITECT
Hellmuth, Obata + Kassabaum
St. Louis, Missouri

RENDERING SIZE
24.5" x 14.5" (62 cm x 37 cm)

MEDIUM
Watercolor

PROJECT
Puerto Madero
Buernos Aires, Argentina

ARCHITECT
Hellmuth, Obata + Kassabaum
St. Louis, Missouri

RENDERING SIZE
15.5" x 10" (39 cm x 25 cm)

MEDIUM
Watercolor

PROJECT
Phillips Arena
Atlanta, Georgia

ARCHITECT
Hellmuth, Obata + Kassabaum
St. Louis, Missouri

RENDERING SIZE
8.5" x 13" (22 cm x 33 cm)

MEDIUM
Watercolor

PROJECT
Gateway Music Museum
East St. Louis, Illinois

ARCHITECT
Gyo Obata and Elysse Newman of
Hellmuth, Obata + Kassabaum
St. Louis, Missouri

RENDERING SIZE
15" x 17" (38 cm x 43 cm)

MEDIUM
Watercolor

LEFT
PROJECT
Ralston Executive Office
St. Louis, Missouri

ARCHITECT
Hellmuth, Obata + Kassabaum
St. Louis, Missouri

RENDERING SIZE
13.5" x 8.5" (33 cm x 22 cm)

MEDIUM
Watercolor

PROJECT
Clayton World Trade Center
Clayton, Missouri

ARCHITECT
Hellmuth, Obata + Kassabaum
St. Louis, Missouri

RENDERING SIZE
10.75" x 12.5" (27 cm x 32 cm)

MEDIUM
Watercolor

AWARDS

*Awards of Excellence in the Graphic
Representation of Architecture; Architecture
in Perspective XI, XII, XIV (1996, 1997, 1999)*

CHARLIE MANUS

ARCHITECTURAL PRESENTATION ARTS   43 UNION AVENUE, #1   MEMPHIS, TENNESSEE 38103   901-525-4335 TEL   901-527-1143 FAX
888-763-3949   EMAIL APAILLUS@AOL.COM

Charlie Manus is a professional architectural illustrator who has provided clients with quality illustrations for nearly thirty years. He not only is extremely sensitive to deadlines and budgets but also offers many styles: pencil, pen and ink, vignettes, and full-color illustrations. Using computer wireframes before final layouts are completed, he insures the proper view. Manus provides illustrations to an ever-expanding, increasingly demanding, and highly regarded list of regional, national, and international clients.

ABOVE
PROJECT
Hampton Inn and Suites
Memphis, Tennessee
ARCHITECT
RTKL Associates
RENDERING SIZE
14" x 22" (36 cm x 56 cm)
MEDIA
Acrylic and gouache

LEFT
PROJECT
Renaissance Center
Memphis, Tennessee
ARCHITECT
Weston Design
RENDERING SIZE
14" x 22" (36 cm x 56 cm)
MEDIA
Acrylic and gouache

PROJECT
Federal Express Hub
Dallas, Texas

ARCHITECT
Taylor & Gardner

RENDERING SIZE
20" x 30" (51 cm x 76 cm)

MEDIA
Acrylic and gouache

ABOVE RIGHT
PROJECT
Jackson Madison General Hospital
Jackson, Tennessee

ARCHITECT
Nathan Evans Taylor Coleman & Foster

RENDERING SIZE
18" x 28" (46 cm x 71 cm)

MEDIA
Acrylic and gouache

RIGHT
PROJECT
Colonnade Building
Memphis, Tennessee

ARCHITECT
Allen & Hoshal, Inc.

RENDERING SIZE
14" x 24" (36 cm x 61 cm)

MEDIA
Acrylic and gouache

BELOW
PROJECT
Chicago City Hospital
Chicago City, Minnesota

ARCHITECT
Jones, Mah, Gaskill, & Rhodes

RENDERING SIZE
18" x 28" (46 cm x 71 cm)

MEDIA
Acrylic and gouache

131

PROJECT
Regional Psychiatric Hospital
Tupelo, Mississippi
ARCHITECT
McCarty & Associates
RENDERING SIZE
14" x 26" (36 cm x 66 cm)
MEDIA
Acrylic and gouache

BELOW
PROJECT
Research Center
Oxford, Mississippi
ARCHITECT
Foil/Wyatt & Associates
RENDERING SIZE
14" x 24" (36 cm x 61 cm)
MEDIA
Acrylic and gouache

PROJECT
Arkansas State University
Mountain Home, Arkansas

ARCHITECT
Wilcox Group

RENDERING SIZE
16" x 28" (41 cm x 71 cm)

MEDIA
Acrylic and gouache

RIGHT
PROJECT
Southwind
Memphis, Tennessee

ARCHITECT
Weston Design

RENDERING SIZE
12" x 18" (30 cm x 46 cm)

MEDIA
Acrylic and gouache

PROJECT
Renaissance Center
Memphis, Tennessee

ARCHITECT
Weston Design

RENDERING SIZE
14" x 22" (36 cm x 56 cm)

MEDIA
Acrylic and gouache

PROJECT
Hilton Inn
Jackson, Mississippi

ARCHITECT
Jackson, Bronson, & Feraci

RENDERING SIZE
18" x 24" (46 cm x 61 cm)

MEDIA
Acrylic and gouache

RIGHT
PROJECT
Kappa Sigma Fraternity House
University of Arkansas
Fayetteville, Arkansas

ARCHITECT
Jack Tucker & Associates

RENDERING SIZE
12" x 18" (30 cm x 46 cm)

MEDIUM
Pen and ink

BELOW RIGHT
PROJECT
Montana Lodge Project
Bozeman, Montana

ARCHITECT
Jerry Locali & Associates

RENDERING SIZE
11" x 17" (28 cm x 43 cm)

MEDIUM
Pencil sketch

PROFESSIONAL AFFILIATIONS

*Past President and Member: American Society
of Architectural Perspectivists*

RAYS TRACED

BY WILLEM VAN DEN HOED

The city of Delft is on the verge of waking up. Virtually the only movement on this early summer morning is that of the sun and her aides-de-camp, the deep blue and purple shadows, traveling slowly over the stones, curbs, window frames, and tiles of the old town. The shadows have soft edges that fall smoothly over the crisp shapes of the buildings.

After a journey of several minutes, a journey that started within the core of the sun, the first strong parallel rays of the morning sunlight reach the closed white curtains of a small bedroom window on the second floor of an old house in the city's center. Neighboring rays light up the deep cadmium orange roof tiles next to the window. The sky is a cold and distant light blue.

When the rays of sunlight reach the white curtain fabric, something peculiar happens. Most of the rays are broken apart and explode into millions of new little bright rays traveling in straight lines in all directions, like bees leaving a hive. Those rays that manage to penetrate the curtains without exploding, one millionth of a second later, bounce onto the dark brown wood of the bedroom floor, leaving there a tracing of the window's skewed shape. A modest number of new brown rays bounce up from the wooden floor and slowly begin to explore the small room. They meet the small bright rays from the curtains that are trying to reach the dark corners of this unknown room. They bounce against walls and explode into minute, new rays that take some of the color of the objects they encounter.

A chaos of multicolored and multidirectional rays of light leaps about the room, trying to pierce the chinks next to the door. Then, a little while later, with the help of some new, strong friends, these rays finally manage to enter the hallway next to the bedroom. And here, after so much work, they fall asleep against the walls that are dimly lit by their presence.

Meanwhile in the bedroom, a few rays have a special mission. They are trying to infiltrate the blankets, to move through the eyelids into the iris, looking for the retina that contains the nerves that will generate small electrical currents to tell my brain to wake up. After a little while, the rays succeed. I get their message and open my eyes, looking squintingly around the room for a moment. I get up slowly and wade through the thick layers of exuberant multidirectional light rays to my studio next door, where my drawing awaits me.

To painters, light is everything—it is what we paint and what we paint with. Therefore, an understanding of the rules governing its behavior is essential. It should be simple enough, since light rays are governed by elementary physics, but the interactions of countless numbers of rays, reflecting, refracting, and deflecting quickly produce complication and confusion. Painters through history have translated these rules onto canvas with varying degrees of success. Now, computers have promised an end to our confusion.

A brief consideration of the nature of light will tell us that it should be incredibly straightforward, but also a little complicated, to simulate light (and, through it, realism) with a computer. Let the computer produce a realistic image of a proposed scene, and you will have a photograph of the future.

The exercise is simple: Accurately define the materials to be shown, and describe their influence on the light rays that will strike them. After striking an opaque surface, each ray will bounce in a perfect mirror image of the original. A perfectly opaque material will reproduce an infinite number of identical rays possessing the same color and traveling in all possible directions. All other materials will have characteristic reflection diagrams that can be defined in a precise way. The computer that will plot these equations needs to be powerful. The light ray that reaches the white curtain by the bedroom window breaks into millions of new rays and multiplies itself in the bedroom into an infinite number of rays with an infinite number of directions and with an infinite number of colors—all within a few bounces.

Light is like a fluid. It fills the smallest holes; every object in a room will get moist from one single lightbulb that is hanging in the middle of the room. It is fascinating to see what happens in the corners of spaces that are not reached by the direct (first-generation) rays from the light source. These corners are illuminated subtly by stray light that bounces off the objects that are lit directly by the light source. Soft brushes of light touch upon these planes, light with intriguing colors coming from unexpected places. The tracing of the bedroom window on the wooden floor is the only direct light, all other visibility results from the complex pattern of indirect light.

Entering the studio next to my bedroom, I touch the computer mouse briefly. The screen comes alive, and after a few seconds, the ventilator and hard disk start to breathe and hum as the computer also wakes up. The screen slowly reveals the image that the computer took part of the night to render. The strawberries!! A rendered image of the design for a market hall in Luxembourg appears on-screen. The hall used to be a railway roundhouse with a circular floor plan. Drawing a round building by hand and in perspective is difficult, but not with a computer: Model one segment and copy thirty-eight times around the centerpoint. The newly designed market stands did not pose a problem either. What had worried me was how to visualize the products that were sold in these stands: bread, meat, fish, bananas, and strawberries. Here, the interplay of light and color would be critical, so I decided to map the product onto the model. I had found good images of fruit, either from magazines or from scanning the fruit directly. Mapping on irregular shapes is hard to do, at least for me— the angles and directions are hard to understand. What I like about mapping, I guess, is that you never quite know what you will get. When I went to bed, with the computer still running, I had not been quite sure about the scale and direction of the strawberry map. I thought the computer would sort it out. What a startling surprise to find the strawberries, perfectly arranged, one per box— huge strawberries, a thousand times enlarged, illogical, formed by chance, but otherwise perfect.

Computers may seem to understand the rules, but they can never work entirely alone. They have no judgment or common sense. If they are well trained, they may produce acceptable perspectives, and that can be very helpful in predicting the future, but we are artists and we want more! We want atmosphere and feeling in our images!

I don't believe that we have to fully understand light in all its complexity. We do not have to explain the incomprehensibilities. In this, we often have to accept and acknowledge illogic. We should even use illogic and chance as tools. Once we experience their great possibilities in refining (actually un-refining) the rendered image, we are on our way. A degree of disrespect for a computer rendering is essential. Even a sophisticated rendering with ninety omnilights, twenty ray-trace reflecting bitmapped materials, and highly detailed modeling will need modification.

The tracing of the window frame on the bedroom floor is simple and logical. Everything else in the room is visible because of the almost fluid nature of indirect light. This means that most of the picture that we perceive inside the room is formed in a way that we cannot completely understand. We cannot determine the path that the light rays have taken to reach the high ceiling. The steamy light rays will not let themselves be understood.

BARBARA MORELLO

MORELLO ART & DESIGN   4936 YONGE STREET, SUITE 167   TORONTO, ONTARIO, CANADA M2N 6S3
416-250-9812/519-272-2696 TEL   519-272-1534 FAX

Barbara Morello, an interior design graduate of Fanshawe College in London, has studied fine arts at both Wilfred Laurier and University of Toronto. Then realizing her talents pertained to the art of architecture, she pursued her career in architectural and interior rendering.

Morello's passion for architecture brought her to Europe for five years, where she honed her skills not only in watercolor painting, but also in oils and in creating large architectural friezes on canvas. With studios in both Toronto and Vienna, Barbara Morello services an international clientele. Fluent in both English and German, she offers fourteen years of experience and devotes herself to the quality of each painting.

ABOVE
PROJECT
Tidelands
Long Beach, California
ARCHITECT
Ehrenkrantz Eckstut and Kuhn PC
New York, New York
RENDERING SIZE
10" x 7" (25 cm x 18 cm)
MEDIUM
Watercolor

This illustration shows a view of Pine Avenue Pier.

LEFT
PROJECT
Tidelands
Long Beach, California
ARCHITECT
Ehrenkrantz Eckstut and Kuhn PC
New York, New York
RENDERING SIZE
10" x 7" (25 cm x 18 cm)
MEDIUM
Watercolor

This illustration shows Tidelands from an aerial view.

PROJECT
Tidelands
Long Beach, California

ARCHITECT
Ehrenkrantz Eckstut and Kuhn PC
New York, New York

RENDERING SIZE
10" x 7" (25 cm x 18 cm)

MEDIUM
Watercolor

This illustration presents a cinematic view.

PROJECT
On Tower Base
Toronto, Ontario, Canada

ARCHITECT
Ehrenkrantz Eckstut and Kuhn PC
New York, New York

RENDERING SIZE
17" x 11" (43 cm x 28 cm)

MEDIUM
Watercolor

RIGHT
PROJECT
Main Post Office
Chicago, Illinois

ARCHITECT
Ehrenkrantz Eckstut and Kuhn PC
New York, New York

RENDERING SIZE
17" x 11" (43 cm x 28 cm)

MEDIUM
Watercolor

This illustration offers a night shot of the
post office.

PROJECT
Main Post Office
Chicago, Illinois

ARCHITECT
Ehrenkrantz Eckstut and Kuhn PC
New York, New York

RENDERING SIZE
17" x 11" (43 cm x 28 cm)

MEDIUM
Watercolor

This illustration provides a morning shot of the post office.

PROJECT
Main Post Office
Chicago, Illinois

ARCHITECT
Ehrenkrantz Eckstut and Kuhn PC
New York, New York

RENDERING SIZE
17" x 11" (43 cm x 28 cm)

MEDIUM
Watercolor

PROJECT
Condo in the Beaches
Toronto, Ontario, Canada

ARCHITECT
Burka Architects
Toronto, Ontario, Canada

RENDERING SIZE
28" x 14" (71 cm x 36 cm)

MEDIUM
Watercolor

This illustration gives a courtyard view.

PROJECT
Condo in the Beaches
Toronto, Ontario, Canada

ARCHITECT
Burka Architects
Toronto, Ontario, Canada

RENDERING SIZE
28" x 18" (71 cm x 46 cm)

MEDIUM
Watercolor
This illustration shows the front entrance.

PROJECT
Condo in the Beaches
Toronto, Ontario, Canada

ARCHITECT
Burka Architects
Toronto, Ontario, Canada

RENDERING SIZE
25" x 20" (54 cm x 51 cm)

MEDIUM
Watercolor

The front entrance is shown here.

PROJECT
Manitoba Telecom System
Winnipeg, Manitoba, Canada

ARCHITECT
Bregmann and Hamann
Toronto, Ontario, Canada

RENDERING SIZE
17" x 11" (43 cm x 28 cm)

MEDIUM
Watercolor

PROJECT
Fairfields Equestrian Centre Home
King, Canada

DESIGNER
Steve McCasey
Aurora, Canada

RENDERING SIZE
26" x 16" (66 cm x 41 cm)

MEDIUM
Watercolor

PROJECT
Housing Project
Staten Island, New York

ARCHITECT
Ehrenkrantz Eckstut and Kuhn PC
New York, New York

RENDERING SIZE
10" x 6" (25 cm x 15 cm)

MEDIUM
Watercolor

PROJECT
Old Airport Redevelopment
Addis Ababa, Ethiopia

ARCHITECT
Skidmore, Owings & Merrill
Chicago, Illinois

RENDERING SIZE
11" x 8" (28 cm x 20 cm)

MEDIUM
Watercolor

This illustration presents a night shot.

PROJECT
Old Airport Redevelopment
Addis Ababa, Ethiopia

ARCHITECT
Skidmore, Owings & Merrill
Chicago, Illinois

RENDERING SIZE
11" x 8" (28 cm x 20 cm)

MEDIUM
Watercolor

This illustration offers a morning shot.

RIGHT
PROJECT
Man on Horse

RENDERING SIZE
42" x 50" (107 cm x 127 cm)

MEDIUM
Oil

This illustration depicts a self-commissioned abstract architectural frieze.

BELOW RIGHT
PROJECT
Il Est Libre

RENDERING SIZE
48" x 29" (122 cm x 74 cm)

MEDIUM
Oil

This is a commissioned copy of the Jean-Jacques Lequeu original.

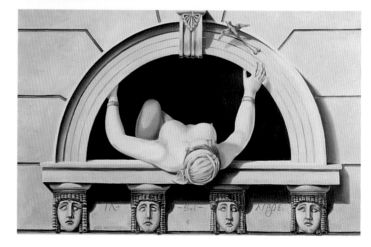

PROJECT
Erotic Architecture
RENDERING SIZE
10" x 14" (25 cm x 36 cm)
MEDIUM
Watercolor

This is a self-commissioned painting.

ABOVE RIGHT
PROJECT
Old Airport Redevelopment
Addis Ababa, Ethiopia
ARCHITECT
Skidmore, Owings & Merrill
Chicago, Illinois
RENDERING SIZE
22" x 34" (56 cm x 86 cm)
MEDIUM
Watercolor

This illustration represents a plan view
of the project.

LEFT
PROJECT
Penn's Landing
Philadelphia, Pennsylvania
ARCHITECT
Ehrenkrantz Eckstut and Kuhn PC
New York, New York
RENDERING SIZE
8" x 11" (20 cm x 28 cm)
MEDIUM
Watercolor

BELOW LEFT
PROJECT
Science City
Kansas City, Missouri
ARCHITECT
Douglas Gallager
Washington, DC
RENDERING SIZE
22" x 24" (56 cm x 61 cm)
MEDIUM
Watercolor

PUBLICATIONS

Art of Architecture book

The Kurier

The Bank Journal

Penthouse

A 3 Boom

ART SHOWS

Private showings to dealers and clients, 1996

*Erotic Art & Architecture, sponsored by Casino
Austria, Baden, Austria, September 1995*

*Aedes Gallery ASAP traveling exhibition, Berlin,
Germany, February 1995*

*Erotic Architecture, sponsored by Fantl
Wirkshaft, GmbH Salzburg, Austria,
December 1994*

*Anton Presoly/Barb Morello exhibit, sponsored
by Anton Presoly, April 1994*

*Architecture and Watercolour, sponsored by
Bank Austria, Vienna, November 1993*

*Architecture and Watercolour, sponsored by
Bank Austria, Vienna, December 1992*

MARK S.C. NELSON, AIA

MARK S.C. NELSON, AIA   DEPARTMENT OF INTERIOR ARCHITECTURE, UNIVERSITY OF WISCONSIN—STEVENS POINT
STEVENS POINT, WISCONSIN 54481   715-346-4034 TEL   NELSONDSGN@AOL.COM
HTTP://MEMBERS.AOL.COM/NELSONDSGN

Mark S.C. Nelson is Assistant Professor of Interior Architecture at the University of Wisconsin–Stevens Point. He has created award-winning design visualization that includes architectural illustration, dynamic imaging, and design. Architectural illustration focuses on the timeless goal of communicating form and emotion through light and shadow. Dynamic imaging portrays motion with animation, digital compositing, and special effects. Design includes graphic design, Website design, and design consulting.

In 1996, 1997, 1998, and 1999 Nelson's illustrations received Awards of Excellence in the American Society of Architectural Perspectivists' international illustration competition. Another illustration received a 1997 Cadalyst Design Visualization Award. *Digital Architecture: Computer Graphics From 50 Top Designers* also features examples of work by Nelson.

Mark S. C. Nelson, AIA, is a licensed architect. He began working as a traditional pen-and-ink illustrator in 1985. Since then, he has been involved with projects from 200 to 2,000,000 square feet (20 to 20,000 square meters) as an illustrator, designer, and architect. Nelson remains committed to developing new illustration techniques and continues to look for new ways to communicate the elusive qualities of a design.

ABOVE

PROJECT
Four Stamford Plaza Lobby
Stamford, Connecticut

CLIENT
Equity Office Properties
Chicago, Illinois

ARCHITECT
ISI
Chicago, Illinois

RENDERING SIZE
28" x 21" (71 cm x 53 cm)

MEDIUM
Computer-generated

In this redesign of an existing office lobby, light and form are delicately modeled in shade and shadow. The illustration was used for leasing purposes.

LEFT

PROJECT
Waterfall with Gazebo
Hoffman Estates, Illinois

CLIENT
National Real Estate
Schaumburg, Illinois

ARCHITECT
Gordon Wigodner Chin & Associates, Ltd.
Northbrook, Illinois

RENDERING SIZE
11" x 8" (28 cm x 20 cm)

MEDIUM
Computer-generated

The illustration shows a proposed waterfall and gazebo for an office park. It was used for a zoning board review. Plants and water cascade down the hill.

PROJECT
Hassel Road Office Park
Hoffman Estates, Illinois

CLIENT
National Real Estate
Schaumburg, Illinois

ARCHITECT
Gordon Wigodner Chin & Associates, Ltd.
Northbrook, Illinois

RENDERING SIZE
40" x 15" (102 cm x 38 cm)

MEDIUM
Computer-generated

The illustration was used to promote a proposed office park.

RIGHT

PROJECT
tax.cch.com
worldwide web

CLIENT
CCH, Inc.
Riverwoods, Illinois

DESIGNER
Mark S.C. Nelson, AIA

RENDERING SIZE
1,259 x 1,528 pixels

MEDIUM
Computer-generated

The illustration is of a "building" that serves as the interface for the company's tax information Website. The owner has populated the rooms with objects that serve as links to other "rooms," or informational areas of the Website.

BELOW RIGHT

PROJECT
High Speed Rail Terminal
Kyungju, South Korea

ARCHITECTS
Anderson & Oh
Chicago, Illinois

RENDERING SIZE
14"x 10" (36 cm x 25 cm)

MEDIUM
Computer-generated

This plaza view shows the rail terminal entrance just after sunrise. It is the centerpiece of a master plan for a new town.

PROJECT
Office Atrium, Electric Power Research Facility
Taejon, South Korea

CLIENT
Haenglim Architects
South Korea

ARCHITECT
Young H. Ki & Associates with
Hanno Weber & Associates
Chicago, Illinois

RENDERING SIZE
16" x 12" (41 cm x 30 cm)

MEDIUM
Computer-generated

The atrium of this proposed research facility reveals pedestrian walkways and bamboo gardens. This preliminary design illustration was used as part of a competition entry.

BELOW LEFT
PROJECT
High Speed Rail Terminal
Kyungju, South Korea

ARCHITECT
Anderson & Oh, Inc.

RENDERING SIZE
14" x 10" (36 cm x 25 cm)

MEDIUM
Computer-generated

This aerial view shows the rail terminal glowing at sunset.

ABOVE RIGHT
PROJECT
Rotunda Building
O'Hare International Airport
Chicago, Illinois

CLIENT
Host Marriott
Chicago, Illinois

ARCHITECT
Gordon Wigodner Chin & Associates, Ltd.
Northbrook, Illinois

RENDERING SIZE
23" x 18" (58 cm x 46 cm)

MEDIUM
Computer-generated

The illustration shows a proposed business travelers' center at a major international airport.

LEFT
PROJECT
Northbrook Court Tenant
Northbrook, Illinois

CLIENT
General Growth Properties
Chicago, Illinois

ARCHITECT
Gordon Wigodner Chin & Associates, Ltd.
Northbrook, Illinois

RENDERING SIZE
16" x 12" (41 cm x 30 cm)

MEDIUM
Digital Ray Tracing composite

Leasing sketch design for a prospective shopping mall tenant.

PROJECT
Dining Area, Electric Power Research Facility
Taejon, South Korea

CLIENT
Haenglim Architects
South Korea

ARCHITECT
Young H. Ki & Associates with
Hanno Weber & Associates
Chicago, Illinois

RENDERING SIZE
16" x 12" (41 cm x 30 cm)

MEDIUM
Computer-generated

The dining area of this facility overlooks a
historic site. This preliminary design illustration
served as part of a competition entry.

PROJECT
Library, Electric Power Research Facility
Taejon, South Korea

CLIENT
Haenglim Architects
South Korea

ARCHITECT
Young H. Ki & Associates with
Hanno Weber & Associates
Chicago, Illinois

RENDERING SIZE
16" x 12" (41 cm x 30 cm)

MEDIUM
Computer-generated

The preliminary design illustration of
this research facility library was part of a
competition entry.

PROJECT
Courtyard, Electric Power Research Facility
Taejon, South Korea

CLIENT
Haenglim Architects
South Korea

ARCHITECT
Young H. Ki & Associates with
Hanno Weber & Associates
Chicago, Illinois

RENDERING SIZE
16" x 12" (41 cm x 30 cm)

MEDIUM
Computer-generated

This view from a research facility office
highlights the exterior courtyard, with atrium
beyond. The preliminary design illustration
was also used as part of a competition entry.

LEFT
PROJECT
Law Office, Elevator Lobby
San Francisco, California

CLIENT
Heller Ehrman White & McAuliffe
San Francisco, California

ARCHITECT
Skidmore, Owings & Merrill LLP

RENDERING SIZE
13" x 10" (33 cm x 25 cm)

MEDIUM
Computer-generated

This illustration of the elevator lobby provides
an example of carefully rendered materials and
lighting atmosphere.

BELOW LEFT
PROJECT
Law Office, Reception Area
San Francisco, California

CLIENT
Heller Ehrman White & McAuliffe
San Francisco, California

ARCHITECT
Skidmore, Owings & Merrill LLP

RENDERING SIZE
13" x 10" (33 cm x 25 cm)

MEDIUM
Computer-generated

In this illustration of the reception area, materials and lighting are rendered to establish the
desired ambience.

PROJECT
Administration Building, Fine Arts School,
Master Plan
Seoul, South Korea

ARCHITECT
Anderson & Oh, Inc.
Chicago, Illinois

RENDERING SIZE
16" x 11" (41 cm x 28 cm)

MEDIUM
Computer-generated

This exterior view shows how the main administration building would be sculpturally shaped
as the centerpiece of the campus.

ABOVE LEFT
PROJECT
Library, Fine Arts School, Master Plan
South Korea

ARCHITECT
Anderson & Oh, Inc.
Chicago, Illinois

RENDERING SIZE
16" x 11" (41 cm x 28 cm)

MEDIUM
Computer-generated

This interior view of the library emphasizes soft
lighting and classic form.

PROJECT
401 N. Aberdeen Condominiums
Chicago, Illinois

CLIENT
Michael Scoby
Chicago, Illinois

DESIGNERS
David MacKenzie
Chicago, Illinois

RENDERING SIZE
16" x 12" (41 cm x 30 cm)

MEDIUM
Computer-generated

This illustration of a proposed luxury condominium
development supported marketing efforts in the
local press.

PROJECT
Arts Club of Chicago
Chicago, Illinois

CLIENT
Self-commissioned

ARCHITECT
Mark S. C. Nelson, AIA
Riverside, Illinois

RENDERING SIZE
18" x 11" (46 cm x 28 cm)

MEDIUM
Computer-generated

This illustration of the proposed alternative design for the Arts Club of Chicago portrays the transparent structure, as seen from the dining area.

LEFT
PROJECT
Arts Club of Chicago
Chicago, Illinois

CLIENT
Self-commissioned

ARCHITECT
Mark S. C. Nelson, AIA
Riverside, Illinois

RENDERING SIZE
13" x 18" (33 cm x 46 cm)

MEDIUM
Computer-generated

The illustration shows a proposed alternative design for the Arts Club of Chicago. This night view portrays the dynamic form and transparency of the structure.

BELOW
PROJECT
Arts Club of Chicago
Chicago, Illinois

CLIENT
Self-commissioned

ARCHITECT
Mark S. C. Nelson, AIA
Riverside, Illinois

RENDERING SIZE
18" x 14" (46 cm x 36 cm)

MEDIUM
Computer-generated

Part of the proposed alternative design for the Arts Club of Chicago, this sketch portrays the dynamic rotunda over the library, with nods to Claes Oldenberg and Coosje van Bruggen.

149

PROFESSIONAL AFFILIATIONS

American Institute of Architects (AIA)

National Trust for Historic Preservation

American Society of Architectural Perspectivists (ASAP)

Riverside Arts Center

Chicago Artists' Coalition

STEVE PARKER

PARKER STUDIOS, INC.   4466 WEST PINE, SUITE 17E   ST. LOUIS, MISSOURI 63108   314-531-8802 TEL   314-531-8602 FAX

Steve Parker has dedicated his talents to the illustration profession since 1979 and has since been honored to participate in numerous national and international exhibits. His work has been featured in major publications and has been recognized with many illustration awards. His expertise in concept design presentation artwork has taken him around the world to work with clients both in-house and at project sites, interacting closely with the project design teams.

Parker's work reflects a creative and confident energy conveyed through an artful balance of style, light, drama, color palette, and composition. "Essentially, my challenge is to express someone else's design vision with my imagination," he says. "The client and I form a true team and together we mold, sculpt, and reform ideas into one clear and commanding visual package. Often this process is as rewarding as doing the artwork itself!"

ABOVE
PROJECT
Anaheim Convention Center Expansion
Anaheim, California
CLIENT
City of Anaheim
ARCHITECT
Steven Brubaker of
Hellmuth Obata + Kassabaum
RENDERING SIZE
12" x 30" (30 cm x 76 cm)
MEDIUM
Prismacolor

LEFT
PROJECT
Abu Dhabi Trade Center
Abu Dhabi, United Arab Emirates
ARCHITECT
William Hellmuth of
Hellmuth Obata + Kassabaum
Washington, DC
RENDERING SIZE
12" x 16" (30 cm x 41 cm)
MEDIUM
Watercolor

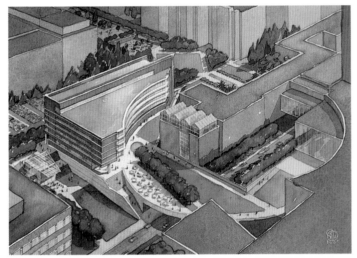

PROJECT
Manugistics Corporate Headquarters
Gaithersburg, Maryland

ARCHITECT
William Hellmuth of
Hellmuth Obata + Kassabaum
Washington, DC

CLIENT
Manugistics, Inc.

RENDERING SIZE
12" x 16" (30 cm x 41 cm)

MEDIUM
Watercolor

152

ABOVE LEFT AND RIGHT
PROJECT
Residential Tower 3 Project
São Paulo, Brazil

CLIENT
CBPO

ARCHITECT
Roger Soto of
Hellmuth Obata + Kassabaum
Houston, Texas

RENDERING SIZE
8" x 14" (20 cm x 36 cm)

MEDIA
Watercolor with Prismacolor

These conceptual studies show an
entry-approach and garden plaza.

LEFT
PROJECT
Pepco Building Proposal
Washington, DC

ARCHITECT
William Hellmuth of
Hellmuth Obata + Kassabaum
Washington, DC

RENDERING SIZE
16" x 20" (41 cm x 51 cm)

MEDIUM
Prismacolor

PROJECT
Boeing Learning Center
St. Louis, Missouri

ARCHITECTS
Gyo Obata and Bill Odell of
Hellmuth Obata + Kassabaum
St. Louis, Missouri

RENDERING SIZE
16" x 22" (41 cm x 56 cm)

MEDIUM
Watercolor

This illustration represents a preliminary
concept submittal, part of a winning entry for a
design competition.

RIGHT
PROJECT
2100 McKinney
Dallas, Texas

CLIENT
Crow Development Company

ARCHITECTS
William Hellmuth and Gordon Gilmore
of Hellmuth Obata + Kassabaum

RENDERING SIZE
19" x 19" (48 cm x 48 cm)

MEDIUM
Watercolor

BELOW LEFT AND RIGHT
PROJECT
Troia Resort Community Competition
Portugal

ARCHITECTS
Pablo Laguarda and John Low of
Hellmuth Obata + Kassabaum
Dallas, Texas

RENDERING SIZE
8" x 10"

MEDIUM
Watercolor

These conceptual studies are part of a winning
entry for a design competition.

153

PROJECT
La Rural Exhibition and Entertainment Center,
Exhibition Corridor Entry
Buenos Aires, Argentina

CLIENT
Ogden Corporation

ARCHITECTS
Pablo Laguarda and Livia Franca of
Hellmuth Obata + Kassabaum
Dallas, Texas

RENDERING SIZE
8" x 10" (20 cm x 25 cm)

MEDIUM
Watercolor

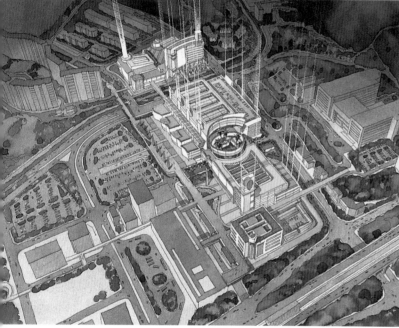

LEFT
PROJECT
Komyoike Regional Center Competition
Osaka, Japan

ARCHITECTS
Pablo Laguarda and John Low of
Hellmuth Obata + Kassabaum
Dallas, Texas

RENDERING SIZE
12" x 15" (30 cm x 38 cm)

MEDIUM
Watercolor

Part of a winning entry for a design competition, this drawing provides an overall view.

ABOVE LEFT
PROJECT
La Rural Exhibition and Entertainment Center,
Exhibition Plaza
Buenos Aires, Argentina

CLIENT
Ogden Corporation

ARCHITECTS
Pablo Laguarda and Livia Franca of
Hellmuth Obata + Kassabaum
Dallas, Texas

RENDERING SIZE
8" x 10" (20 cm x 25 cm)

MEDIUM
Watercolor

PROJECT
Redevelopment Center Competition
Chiba, Japan

ARCHITECTS
Pablo Laguarda and John Low of
Hellmuth Obata + Kassabaum
Dallas, Texas

RENDERING SIZE
8" x 8" (20 cm x 20 cm)

MEDIUM
Watercolor

Part of a winning entry for a design competition
presents a vignette of Retail Pier.

PROJECT
BJC Medical Center
St. Louis, Missouri

ARCHITECTS
Gyo Obata and Hank Winkelman of
Hellmuth Obata + Kassabaum
St. Louis, Missouri

RENDERING SIZE
12" x 16" (30 cm x 41 cm)

MEDIUM
Watercolor

RIGHT AND BELOW
PROJECT
Sun Microsystems Campus Walk-Through series
Broomfield, Colorado

CLIENT
Sun Microsystems

ARCHITECT
Bill Odell of
Hellmuth Obata + Kassabaum
St. Louis, Missouri

RENDERING SIZE
12" x 18"

MEDIA
Sepia ink and Prismacolor

Three views of office complex park.

155

AWARDS

*Best Sketch Category Award: Architecture in
Perspective XII, 1997*

*Awards of Excellence in the Graphic
Representation of Architecture*

Architecture in Perspective 6, 7, 9, 10, 11, 14

GUANG HAO QIAN

G.H. QIAN STUDIO   128 ELLIS PARK   TORONTO, ONTARIO, CANADA M6S 2V5   416-769-5987 TEL   416-769-7155 FAX

Guanghao Qian had practiced as an architect for six years. Since 1991, he has gradually established his reputation as an architectural illustrator internationally. Awards he's won include the Special Gold Prize (Award of the Minister of Construction of the Japanese government) in Nagoya International Public Design Competition 1988; the Formal Category Winner of the Architecture in Perspective 13 1998; and the Award of Excellence of the Architecture in Perspective 14 1999.

ABOVE
PROJECT
Uptown Core Park
Oakville, Ontario, Canada
ARCHITECTS
Kuwabara Payne McKenna Blumberg Architects
Milus Bollenberghe Topps Watchorn
Environmental Artworks
RENDERING SIZE
14" x 10" (36 cm x 25 cm)
MEDIUM
Watercolor

RIGHT
PROJECT
Urban Design Guideline for the
Newmarket Regional Centre
Newmarket, Ontario, Canada
ARCHITECT
Baird/Sampson
RENDERING SIZE
26" x 15" (66 cm x 38 cm)
MEDIUM
Watercolor

This illustration was the Formal Category Winner of the Architecture in Perspective 13 Competition.

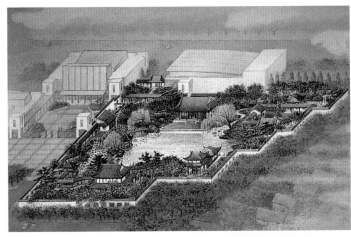

ABOVE LEFT

PROJECT
Chinese Cultural Centre
Scarborough, Ontario, Canada

ARCHITECTS
Kuwabara Payne McKenna Blumberg Architects
Patrick T. Y. Chan, Architect

RENDERING SIZE
15" x 30" (38 cm x 76 cm)

MEDIUM
Watercolor

ABOVE RIGHT

PROJECT
Rahimi Developments
Hamburg, Germany

ARCHITECT
Kuwabara Payne McKenna Blumberg Architects

RENDERING SIZE
11" x 17" (28 cm x 43 cm)

MEDIUM
Watercolor

RIGHT

PROJECT
Hummingbird Centre
Toronto, Ontario, Canada

ARCHITECT
Kuwabara Payne McKenna Blumberg Architects

RENDERING SIZE
9" x12" (23 cm x 30 cm)

MEDIUM
Watercolor

PROJECT
500 Queen's Quay West Condominiums
Toronto, Ontario, Canada

ARCHITECT
Kuwabara Payne McKenna Blumberg Architects

RENDERING SIZE
10" x 14" (25 cm x 36 cm)

MEDIUM
Watercolor

Guanghao Qian 95.

PROJECT
500 Queen's Quay West Condominium
Toronto, Ontario, Canada

ARCHITECT
Kuwabara Payne McKenna Blumberg Architects

RENDERING SIZE
11" x 17" (28 cm x 43 cm)

MEDIUM
Watercolor

ABOVE LEFT
PROJECT
Soho Street Condominiums
Toronto, Ontario, Canada

ARCHITECT
Kuwabara Payne McKenna Blumberg Architects

RENDERING SIZE
10" x 14" (25 cm x 36 cm)

MEDIUM
Watercolor

LEFT
PROJECT
Opera House
Toronto, Ontario, Canada

ARCHITECT
Kuwabara Payne McKenna Blumberg Architects

RENDERING SIZE
8.5" x 11" (22 cm x 28 cm)

MEDIUM
Watercolor

PROJECT
Goodman Theatre
Chicago, Illinois

ARCHITECT
Kuwabara Payne McKenna Blumberg Architects

RENDERING SIZE
10.5" x 17" (27 cm x 43 cm)

MEDIUM
Watercolor

PROJECT
Munk Centre for International Studies
Toronto, Ontario, Canada

ARCHITECT
Kuwabara Payne McKenna Blumberg Architects

RENDERING SIZE
9" x 15" (23 cm x 38 cm)

MEDIUM
Watercolor

PROJECT
500 Queen's Quay West Condominiums
Toronto, Ontario, Canada

ARCHITECT
Kuwabara Payne McKenna Blumberg Architects

RENDERING SIZE
10" x 18" (25 cm x 46 cm)

MEDIUM
Watercolor

159

PROJECT
National Museum of Saudi Arabia,
Riyadh, Saudi Arabia

ARCHITECT
Moriyama & Teshima Architects

RENDERING SIZE
11" x 17" (28 cm x 43 cm)

MEDIUM
Watercolor

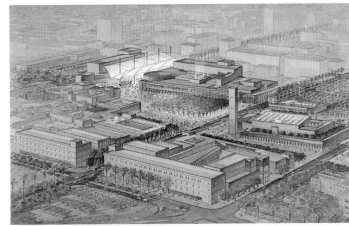

PROJECT
National Museum of Saudi Arabia
Riyadh, Saudi Arabia

ARCHITECT
Moriyama & Teshima Architects

RENDERING SIZE
11" x 17" (28 cm x 43 cm)

MEDIUM
Watercolor

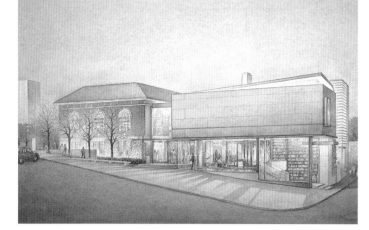

PROJECT
MacLauren Art Centre
Barrie, Ontario, Canada
ARCHITECT
Taylor Hariri Pontarini Architects
RENDERING SIZE
10" x 16" (25 cm x 41 cm)
MEDIUM
Watercolor

PROJECT
Uptown Core Park
Oakville, Ontario, Canada
ARCHITECTS
Kuwabara Payne McKenna Blumberg Architects
Milus Bollenberghe Topps Watchorn
Environmental Artworks
RENDERING SIZE
14" x 10" (36 cm x 25 cm)
MEDIUM
Watercolor

PROJECT
Private Residence,
Richmond Hill, Ontario, Canada
ARCHITECT
Kuwabara Payne McKenna Blumberg Architects
RENDERING SIZE
9.5" x 15" (24 cm x 38 cm)
MEDIUM
Watercolor

PROJECT
Royal Conservatory of Music
Toronto, Ontario, Canada
ARCHITECT
Kuwabara Payne McKenna Blumberg Architects
RENDERING SIZE
10" x 14" (25 cm x 36 cm)
MEDIUM
Watercolor

PROJECT
Canadian Embassy
Berlin, Germany

ARCHITECT
Kuwabara Payne McKenna Blumberg Architects

RENDERING SIZE
9" x 17" (23 cm x 43 cm)

MEDIUM
Watercolor

RIGHT
PROJECT
Trinity College, University of Toronto
Toronto, Ontario, Canada

ARCHITECT
Kuwabara Payne McKenna Blumberg Architects

RENDERING SIZE
17" x 10" (43 cm x 25 cm)

MEDIUM
Watercolor

BELOW
PROJECT
University of Minnesota, Master Plan
Minneapolis, Minnesota

ARCHITECT
Kuwabara Payne McKenna Blumberg Architects

RENDERING SIZE
10" x 17" (25 cm x 43 cm)

MEDIUM
Watercolor

BARBARA WORTH RATNER, AIA

828 CHARLES ALLEN DRIVE, NE   ATLANTA, GEORGIA 30308   404-876-3943 TEL   404-876-0635 FAX   RATZ@MINDSPRING.COM

Barbara Worth Ratner offers a wide and flexible range of illustration techniques. She works closely with client-collaborators toward artistically successful, realistic, and often unique solutions to each problem presented. Watercolor is her primary medium, but she has produced successful images in acrylics, ink, colored pencil, and even cut Pantone film.

To her portfolio of techniques, Ratner adds a special emphasis on the presentation of human figures within architectural settings. As a result, she is often called on for retail, educational, and recreational projects, including a long series of venue illustrations in connection with the 1996 and 2004 Summer Olympic Games.

Barbara Ratner, a member of the Guild of Natural Science Illustrators, has recently had the pleasure and privilege of combining wildlife, human figure, and architectural elements in an extended collection of images for a state-of-the-art zoo expansion.

ABOVE
PROJECT
Cheju International Country Club
and Resort Hotel
Cheju, Korea

ARCHITECT
Thompson, Ventulett, Stainback & Associates
Atlanta, Georgia

RENDERING SIZE
14" x 12" (36 cm x 30 cm)

MEDIUM
Watercolor

LEFT
PROJECT
Cheju International Country Club
and Resort Hotel
Cheju, South Korea

ARCHITECT
Thompson, Ventulett, Stainback & Associates
Atlanta, Georgia

RENDERING SIZE
14" x 11" (36 cm x 28 cm)

MEDIUM
Watercolor

PROJECT
The Shops at Wave Place
Bangkok, Thailand

ARCHITECT
FRCH Design Worldwide
Cincinnati, Ohio

RENDERING SIZE
18" x 25" (46 cm x 64 cm)

MEDIA
Watercolor and ink

RIGHT
PROJECT
Ciro's Plaza
Shanghai, China

ARCHITECT
FRCH Design Worldwide
Cincinnati, Ohio

RENDERING SIZE
11" x 17" (28 cm x 43 cm)

MEDIA
Watercolor and ink

PROJECT
The Great Northwest Exhibit, Oregon Zoo
Portland, Oregon

ARCHITECT
The Portico Group
Seattle, Washington

RENDERING SIZES
Sea Lions, 12" x 14" (30 cm x 36 cm);
Kelp, 9" x 11" (23 cm x 28 cm);
Cougar, 11" x 11" (28 cm x 28 cm);
Bear, 11" x 11" (28 cm x 28 cm);
Salmon/Eagle, 14" x 10" (36 cm x 25 cm);
Otter, 10" x 10" (25 cm x 25 cm)

MEDIA
Watercolor, ink, and pencil

PROJECT
Manufacturing Related Disciplines Complex,
Building III, Georgia Institute of Technology
Atlanta, Georgia

ARCHITECT
Perkins & Will
Atlanta, Georgia

RENDERING SIZE
21" x 15" (53 cm x 38 cm)

MEDIA
Watercolor and ink

PROJECT
North Campus Student Housing,
Brevard College
Brevard, North Carolina

ARCHITECT
Lord, Aeck & Sargent, Architects
Atlanta, Georgia

RENDERING SIZE
18" x 8" (46 cm x 20 cm)

MEDIUM
Watercolor

PROJECT
Piedmont Park Visitor Center, Renovation
Atlanta, Georgia

ARCHITECT
Smith Dalia Architects
Atlanta, Georgia

RENDERING SIZE
12" x 5" (30 cm x 13 cm)

MEDIUM
Watercolor

RIGHT
PROJECT
College of Education,
Georgia Southern University
Statesboro, Georgia

ARCHITECT
The Woodhurst Partnership and
John C. Portman, Jr.
Augusta & Atlanta, Georgia

RENDERING SIZE
25" x 15" (64 cm x 38 cm)

MEDIA
Watercolor and ink

LEFT
PROJECT
North Campus Student Housing,
Brevard College
Brevard, North Carolina

ARCHITECT
Lord, Aeck & Sargent, Architects
Atlanta, Georgia

RENDERING SIZE
Detail, 3" x 8" (8 cm x 20 cm)

MEDIUM
Watercolor

PROJECT
Marriott Hotel Study Prototype

ARCHITECT
CGLS Architects
Atlanta, Georgia

RENDERING SIZE
18" x 10" (46 cm x 25 cm)

MEDIUM
Watercolor

MICHAEL REARDON

MICHAEL REARDON ARCHITECTURAL ILLUSTRATION 5433 BOYD AVENUE   OAKLAND, CALIFORNIA 94618   510-655-7030 TEL

Dynamic architectural drawings are a result of successful design collaboration between client and artist. For more than two decades, Michael Reardon has provided such artwork worldwide. These award-winning illustrations are known for their graceful compositions, luminous color, evocative imagery, and technical elegance.

THIS PAGE
PROJECT
Nilai Corporate Center
Kuala Lumpur, Malaysia

ARCHITECT
Kaplan McLaughlin Diaz
San Francisco, California

MEDIUM
Watercolor

OPPOSITE
PROJECT
Roxas Triangle
Manila, Philippines

ARCHITECT
Skidmore, Owings & Merrill Architects
San Francisco, California

MEDIUM
Watercolor

PROJECT
Travel Sketches
Venice, Italy
MEDIUM
Watercolor

170

PROJECT
Farmer's Market
Los Angeles, California
ARCHITECT
Kaplan McLaughlin Diaz
San Francisco, California
MEDIUM
Watercolor

BELOW
PROJECT
The Port of Phoenice
Marsa Alam, Egypt

ARCHITECT
Wimberly Allison Tong & Goo
London, England

MEDIUM
Watercolor

RIGHT
PROJECT
Xing Guo Hotel
Shanghai, China

ARCHITECT
Hellmuth, Obata + Kassabaum
San Francisco, California

MEDIUM
Watercolor

171

ABOVE
PROJECT
Pantai Mutiara
Jakarta, Indonesia

ARCHITECT
Wimberly Allison Tong & Goo
Honolulu, Hawaii

MEDIUM
Watercolor

ABOVE RIGHT
PROJECT
Stanford Ambulatory Care Center,
Stanford University
Palo Alto, California

ARCHITECT
Kaplan McLaughlin Diaz
San Francisco, California

MEDIUM
Watercolor

RIGHT
PROJECT
Baywood Canyon
Fairfax, California

ARCHITECT
Backen Arrigoni & Ross
San Francisco, California

MEDIUM
Watercolor

PROJECT
Maihama
Tokyo, Japan

ARCHITECT
Paul Ma Design
Emeryville, California

MEDIUM
Pencil

PROJECT
Tamarind Grove Conference Center
Bangalore, India

ARCHITECT
Wimberly Allison Tong & Goo
Honolulu, Hawaii

MEDIUM
Pencil

BELOW
PROJECT
Sun Microsystems
Santa Clara, California

ARCHITECT
Hellmuth, Obata + Kassabaum
San Francisco, California

MEDIUM
Pencil

172

LEFT
PROJECT
E & O Hotel
Penang, Malaysia

ARCHITECT
Wimberly Allison Tong & Goo
Honolulu, Hawaii

MEDIUM
Pencil

ABOVE AND RIGHT
PROJECT
Yerba Buena Tower
San Francisco, California

ARCHITECT
Gary Handel and Associates
San Francisco, California

MEDIUM
Watercolor

BELOW
PROJECT
Roatan Resort
Roatan Island, Honduras

ARCHITECT
House and House, Architects
San Francisco, California

MEDIUM
Watercolor

173

ABOVE
PROJECT
Muvico Egyptian Theatre
Davies, Florida

ARCHITECT
Development Design Group
Baltimore, Maryland

MEDIUM
Watercolor

LEFT
PROJECT
Ferry Building Plaza
San Francisco, California

ARCHITECT
ROMA Design Group
San Francisco, California

MEDIUM
Watercolor

RICHARD ROCHON

ROCHON ASSOCIATES 15200 EAST JEFFERSON AVENUE, SUITE 102   GROSSE POINTE PARK, MICHIGAN 48230   313-331-4410 TEL   313-331-4408 FAX

Richard Rochon reflects thirty-seven years of experience in each of his illustrations. His colored pencil technique continues to develop a character well suited for a variety of projects. His styles range from loose conceptual drawings to finely detailed images. Rochon communicates closely with the client to portray each design effectively with the appropriate atmosphere and level of detail.

Rochon Associates' works have been published in a variety of books and featured in other media. Illustrations from projects commissioned by international as well as local clients, along with a brochure of other select illustrations, are available.

ABOVE
PROJECT
Gulf Western Refurbish Proposal
New York, New York
ARCHITECT
Skidmore, Owings & Merrill
New York, New York
MEDIUM
Wax pencil on drafting film

BELOW
PROJECT
West Village/Bluewater Kent
Kent, England
ARCHITECTS
James P. Ryan Associates
Farmington Hills, Michigan
Eric Kuhn
New York, New York
MEDIUM
Wax pencil on drafting film

PROJECT
10 St. James Place
Boston, Massachusetts

ARCHITECT
Skidmore, Owings & Merrill
New York, New York

MEDIUM
Wax pencil on drafting film

PROJECT
Pacific Trade Center
Los Angeles, California

ARCHITECT
Hellmuth, Obata + Kassabaum
St. Louis, Missouri

MEDIUM
Wax pencil on drafting film

LEFT
PROJECT
Battery Park
New York, New York

ARCHITECT
Richard Cook
New York, New York

MEDIUM
Wax pencil on drafting film

PROJECT
Carpenter's Plaza
Detroit, Michigan

ARCHITECT
Shrem/Luttermoser Architects
Southfield, Michigan

176

PROJECT
Lawrence Technological University
Southfield, Michigan

ARCHITECTS
Gwathmey Siegel
New York, New York
Neumann/Smith Associates
Southfield, Michigan

LEFT
PROJECT
Detroit Opera House
Detroit, Michigan

ARCHITECT
James P. Ryan Associates
Farmington Hills, Michigan

177

PROJECT
USTA National Tennis Center
Flushing Meadows, New York

ARCHITECT
Rossetti Associates
Birmingham, Michigan

PROJECT
Stanford University
Palo Alto, California

ARCHITECT
Pei Cobb Freed & Partners
New York, New York

MEDIUM
Wax pencil on vellum

LEFT
PROJECT
1801 North Lynn
Rosslyn, Virginia

ARCHITECT
RTKL Associates
Washington, DC

MEDIUM
Wax pencil on drafting film

BELOW LEFT
PROJECT
Office Tower Proposal
St. Louis, Missouri

ARCHITECT
Hellmuth, Obata + Kassabaum
St. Louis, Missouri

MEDIUM
Wax pencil on drafting film

BELOW RIGHT
PROJECT
Van Ness Residential
San Francisco, California

ARCHITECT
Skidmore, Owings
San Francisco, California

MEDIUM
Wax pencil on drafting film

RIGHT
PROJECT
Mixed Use Development
Turkey

ARCHITECT
Hellmuth, Obata + Kassabaum
St. Louis, Missouri

MEDIUM
Wax pencil on drafting film

ARCHITECT
All Skidmore, Owings & Merrill
except left:
Skidmore, Owings & Merrill
with Frank Gehry and Ricardo Legorreta

ART ASSOCIATES, INC.

RON ROSE   4635 WEST ALEXIS ROAD   TOLEDO, OHIO 43623   419-537-1303 TEL   419-474-9113 FAX

Art Associates has been actively serving a discriminating international clientele since 1966. The skilled staff of artists, architects, designers, computer operators, photographic printers, and model builders has completed more than 25,000 commissions.

Highly respected throughout the field, Art Associates has set the standard for over thirty-two years for dependable service, accuracy, and dedication to capturing the essence of every project.

From the simplest freehand sketch to the very finest, highly detailed presentation, firms of every size repeatedly select Art Associates to express their designs. Art Associates' tireless efforts and pure love of art have resulted in an appreciation of high-quality illustration.

ABOVE
ARCHITECT
Nichols Partnership
RENDERING SIZE
24" x 26" (61 cm x 66 cm)
MEDIUM
Casein style #6

BELOW
ARCHITECT
The Sieger Partnership
RENDERING SIZE
30" x 17" (76 cm x 43 cm)
MEDIUM
Casein style #6

OPPOSITE
PROJECT
World of Wonder Amusement Structure
Vienna, Austria
RENDERING SIZE
30" x 19" (76 cm x 48 cm)
MEDIA
Casein style #6; activity added digitally, animated in real time for promotional video

ABOVE
ARCHITECT
C.Y. Lee

RENDERING SIZE
20" x 32" (51 cm x 81 cm)

MEDIUM
Casein style #6

BELOW
ARCHITECT
Smallwood, Reynolds, Stewart & Stewart
DMJM, Jakarta, Indonesia

RENDERING SIZE
18" x 18" (46 cm x 46 cm)

MEDIUM
Casein style #6

ARCHITECT
Trahan Architects

RENDERING SIZE
13" x 22" (33 cm x 56 cm)

MEDIUM
Casein style #6

ARCHITECT
Projects International

RENDERING SIZE
12" x 20" (30 cm x 51 cm)

MEDIUM
Casein style #6

BELOW
ARCHITECT
Fullerton Diaz

RENDERING SIZE
28" x 31" (71 cm x 79 cm)

MEDIUM
Casein style #6

ARCHITECT
Lund Associates

RENDERING SIZE
27" x 27" (69 cm x 69 cm)

MEDIUM
Casein style #4b

ARCHITECT
Beer Silverstein

RENDERING SIZE
21" x 28" (53 cm x 71 cm)

MEDIUM
Berber style #4b

BELOW
ARCHITECT
Smallwood, Reynolds, Stewart & Stewart
DMJM, Jakarta, Indonesia

RENDERING SIZE
23" x 26" (58 cm x 66 cm)

MEDIUM
Casein style #6

ABOVE
ARCHITECT
United Landmark

RENDERING SIZE
12" x 17" (30 cm x 43 cm)

MEDIUM
Casein style #4b

BELOW
ARCHITECT
Herbert Beckhard/Frank Bachlan Associates

RENDERING SIZE
10" x 16" (25 cm x 41 cm)

MEDIA
Ink line and watercolor style #3b

ABOVE
ARCHITECT
Smallwood, Reynolds, Stewart & Stewart

RENDERING SIZE
18" x 18" (46 cm x 46 cm)

MEDIA
Casein style #6

BELOW
ARCHITECT
Fugate Agency

RENDERING SIZE
12" x 19" (30 cm x 48 cm)

MEDIUM
Casein and watercolor

185

BELOW LEFT
ARCHITECT
Archimage Architectural Consultants

RENDERING SIZE
20" x 26" (51 cm x 66 cm)

MEDIUM
Casein style #6

BELOW
ARCHITECT
Swire Properties

RENDERING SIZE
19" x 22" (48 cm x 56 cm)

MEDIUM
Casein style #6

THOMAS W. SCHALLER, AIA

2112 BROADWAY, #407   NEW YORK, NEW YORK 10023   212-362-5524 TEL   212-362-5719 FAX ARCHPER@AOL.COM

A great deal of successful architectural practice today is marked by a distinctly collaborative approach. More than ever, the disciplines of design, development, and presentation are allowed—even encouraged—to overlap and to interact. In this context, much of Thomas Schaller's recent work is characterized by an emphasis on the visual process of design rather than on the eventual product.

While fully articulated and finished illustration work is still in demand, it is the architectural perspectivist's ability to work as a component of a larger team that has become of increased necessity. A facility for producing hand-drawn development sketches is crucial in maintaining the spontaneous, intuitive character of the architectural design process. Working closely with development clients, as well as with other architects, artists, and diverse creative professionals, has expanded the potential for uniquely effective solutions to many design problems.

ABOVE
PROJECT
Public Library of Nashville and Davidson County,
Proposed Main Reading Room
Nashville, Tennessee
ARCHITECT
Robert A. M. Stern Architects
New York, New York
RENDERING SIZE
20" x 30" (51 cm x 76 cm)
MEDIUM
Watercolor

BELOW LEFT
PROJECT
Proposed Theater for the Academy of Motion
Picture Arts and Sciences
Los Angeles, California
ARCHITECT
Rockwellgroup
New York, New York
RENDERING SIZE
24" x 18" (61 cm x 45 cm)
MEDIUM
Watercolor

BELOW RIGHT
PROJECT
Sultan's Palace, Proposed Lobby
Las Vegas, Nevada
CLIENTS
Trizec Hahn Development Corp.
San Diego, California
Rockwellgroup
New York, New York
ARCHITECT
Rockwellgroup with Todd Oldham
New York, New York
RENDERING SIZE
17" x 11" (43 cm x 28 cm)
MEDIUM
Watercolor

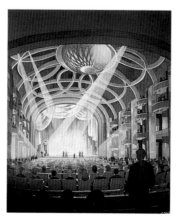

ABOVE RIGHT
PROJECT
The Odyssey Project

CLIENT
The Otis Elevator Company
Hartford, Connecticut

ARCHITECT
Frank Lloyd Wright and Others

RENDERING SIZE
24" x 36" (61 cm x 91 cm)

MEDIUM
Watercolor

RIGHT
PROJECT
The New York Coliseum Site at
Columbus Circle Competition
New York, New York

CLIENT
Millennium Development
New York, New York

ARCHITECTS
J. S. Polshek and Partners
New York, New York
Gary Handel and Associates
New York, New York

RENDERING SIZE
18" x 12" (46 cm x 30 cm)

MEDIA
Graphite pencil and watercolor

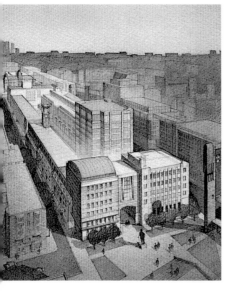

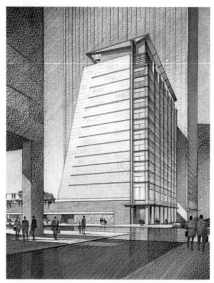

FAR LEFT

PROJECT
University of Pennsylvania,
Proposed Master Plan for Revlon Campus
Philadelphia, Pennsylvania

ARCHITECT
Kohn Pedersen Fox Associates, P.C.
New York, New York

RENDERING SIZE
10" x 10" (25 cm x 25 cm)

MEDIA
Graphite pencil and watercolor

LEFT

PROJECT
Proposed Sports Facility

ARCHITECT
Ellerbe Becket
Kansas City, Missouri

RENDERING SIZE
12" x 18" (30 cm x 46 cm)

MEDIUM
Watercolor

FAR LEFT

PROJECT
Proposed Riverfront Development
Shanghai, China

ARCHITECT
Fox & Fowle
New York, New York

RENDERING SIZE
11" x 17" (28 cm x 43 cm)

MEDIA
Graphite pencil and watercolor

LEFT

PROJECT
55 Water Street
New York, New York

CLIENT
Kohn Pedersen Fox Associates
New York, New York

RENDERING SIZE
10" x 10" (25 cm x 25 cm)

MEDIA
Graphite pencil and watercolor

PROJECT
Hotel "W," View of Proposed Lobby
New York, New York

ARCHITECT
Rockwellgroup
New York, New York

RENDERING SIZE
12" x 18" (30 cm x 46 cm)

MEDIUM
Watercolor

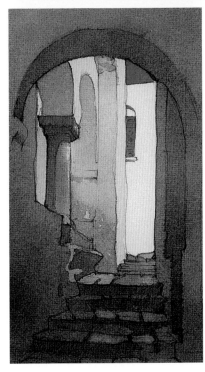

LEFT

PROJECT
Cirque du Soleil
Orlando, Florida

ARCHITECT
Rockwellgroup
New York, New York

RENDERING SIZE
20" x 16" (51 cm x 41 cm)

MEDIUM
Watercolor

BELOW LEFT

PROJECT
Desert Passage, Proposed Gateway
Las Vegas, Nevada

CLIENT
Trizec Hahn Development Corp.
San Diego, California

ARCHITECT
RTKL Associates

RENDERING SIZE
21" x 15" (53 cm x 38 cm)

MEDIUM
Watercolor

This image was illustrated by Douglas E.
Jamieson, Curtis James Woodhouse, and Thomas
Schaller, who also contributed to project design.

BELOW RIGHT

PROJECT
Desert Passage, Proposed "Lost City"
Las Vegas, Nevada

CLIENT
Trizec Hahn Development Corp.
San Diego, California

ARCHITECT
RTKL Associates

RENDERING SIZE
21" x 15" (53 cm x 38 cm)

MEDIUM
Watercolor

This image was illustrated by Douglas E.
Jamieson, Curtis J. Woodhouse, and Thomas
Schaller, who also contributed to project design.

RIGHT
PROJECT
Proposed "E-Walk" Development
New York, New York

CLIENT
Tishman Development Corporation

DESIGN
Arquitectonica
Miami, Florida
Rockwellgroup
New York, New York
Others

ARCHITECTS
Arquitectonica (tower)
Miami, Florida
Rockwellgroup (theater)
New York, New York

RENDERING SIZE
30" x 20" (76 cm x 51 cm)

MEDIUM
Watercolor

BELOW RIGHT
PROJECT
Development for Hong Kong
Harbor Competition

ARCHITECT
Cesar Pelli and Associates
New Haven, Connecticut

RENDERING SIZE
18" x 24" (46 cm x 61 cm)

MEDIUM
Watercolor

HISAE SHODA

SHODA HISAE ATELIER   23-2-206 TAKAMIYA-SHINMACHI NEYAGAWA, OSAKA, JAPAN 572-0847   81-720-21-3212 TEL

Born in Osaka, Japan, Hisae Shoda began a career in architectural rendering in 1991 and joined the American Society of Architectural Perspectivists in 1994. Shoda's goal is to portray the architect's vision through imagery created within a context. Shoda's drawings render the architectural project not only as an independent structure but also as an atmospheric environment complete with wind and light, the sight of gathering people, even the hint of people's voices. Shoda believes that such work can be realized only by cooperating with the architect. The artist can't create illustrations merely by reading plans and schema; creation is a collaborative process. Shoda hopes to better realize the architecture through the image she draws. Even the most beautifully rendered image is ineffective if the architectural vision is not realized.

ABOVE
PROJECT
A-O Project (Day)
ARCHITECT
Takenaka Corporation
RENDERING SIZE
35" x 16" (89 cm x 41 cm)
MEDIA
Computer-generated image with colored pencil

BELOW
PROJECT
K-Theological School #1
ARCHITECT
Takenaka Corporation
RENDERING SIZE
9.5" x 24" (24 cm x 61 cm)
MEDIA
Watercolor and colored pencil

PROJECT
Official Residence of the President of Enno-Kyo

ARCHITECT
Takenaka Corporation

RENDERING SIZE
40" x 26" (102 cm x 66 cm)

MEDIA
Watercolor and pastel

Winner of an 1994 AIP Award of Excellence, this work, with its serene and extensive frame, represents the religious disposition of the facility. The visual style resembles nihon-ga, a complex Japanese painting technique involving powdered mineral pigments. The technique is not appropriate for building renderings that need to be finished within a limited time, so the nihon-ga effect was approximated with watercolor and pastels.

ABOVE RIGHT
PROJECT
A-O Project (Night)

ARCHITECT
Takenaka Corporation

RENDERING SIZE
35" x 16" (89 cm x 41 cm)

MEDIA
Computer-generated image with colored pencil

The two large towers rising into the sky are radio antennas. The colored pencil on the digital image print emphasizes wave and light.

RIGHT
PROJECT
O-Project

ARCHITECT
Takenaka Corporation

RENDERING SIZE
16" x 20" (41 cm x 51 cm)

MEDIA
Pastel and colored pencil

This work illustrates a conference room. Restrained color draws attention to the lighting.

PROJECT
HEP Five Project

ARCHITECT
Takenaka Corporation

RENDERING SIZE
28" x 20" (71 cm x 51 cm)

MEDIA
Airbrush and acrylic

This illustration won the 1996 AIP Formal Category Award. This work represented a department store built in the center of Osaka, the second largest city in Japan. The artist studied possible angles for the drawing many times, hoping to include the big Ferris wheel when rendering the building. The artist decided that the view from a point on the railroad near the site was best.

BELOW
PROJECT
The Walnut School

ARCHITECT
Takenaka Corporation

RENDERING SIZE
8" x 24" (20 cm x 61 cm)

MEDIUM
Colored pencil

This rendering was prepared for entry in a competition. The use of colored pencil creates a sensitive background of light, water, sky, and mountain.

PROJECT
Training Institute and Factory

ARCHITECT
Takenaka Corporation

RENDERING SIZE
16" x 24" (41 cm x 61 cm)

MEDIUM
Watercolor

PROJECT
Kantan House

ARCHITECT
Naoyuki Nagata/I.C.U.

RENDERING SIZE
26" x 17" (66 cm x 43 cm)

MEDIUM
Acrylic

The artist's use of a painting knife and acrylic is inspired by the strong touch of oil painting. The transparent architecture and rough touch offer an interesting contrast.

PROJECT
Mycal Ohmi-Hachiman

ARCHITECT
Hazama Corporation

RENDERING SIZE
19" x 29" (48 cm x 74 cm)

MEDIA
Pen, ink, and watercolor

This rendering, which shows a theater complex, shopping center, amusement palace, and sports gym, features the artist's intricately hand-penned detail.

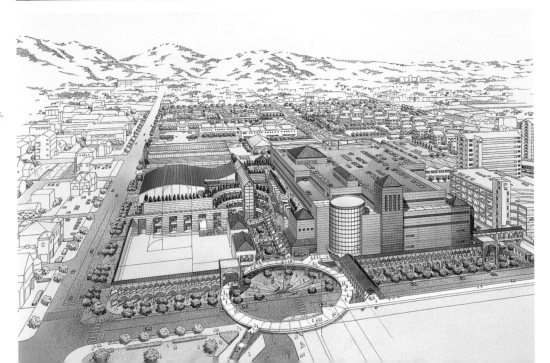

PROJECT
K-Hotel, Restaurant

ARCHITECT
Ogawa Architects & Engineers

RENDERING SIZE
10" x 14" (25 cm x 36 cm)

MEDIA
Pen and ink, and pastel

PROJECT
A-Parking Area

ARCHITECT
Ogawa Architects & Engineers

RENDERING SIZE
11.5" x 16" (29 cm x 41 cm)

MEDIUM
Watercolor

This rendering was prepared part of an entry
for a parking-area competition. The architect
requested a rendered image of a lighted box
floating in darkness.

196

PROJECT
Gymnasium

ARCHITECT
Issey Sugihara/RUI Architects + Engineers
& Associates
Osaka, Japan

RENDERING SIZE
14" x 11.5" (36 cm x 29 cm)

MEDIA
Watercolor and pastel

As an early design-phase presentation, the
image, instead of expressing architectural
details, emphasizes the unanimity of the
building volume and the natural surroundings.

PROJECT
A-Hotel, Entrance

ARCHITECT
RUI Architects + Engineers & Associates
Osaka, Japan

RENDERING SIZE
11.5" x 16" (29 cm x 41 cm)

MEDIA
Airbrush and watercolor

RIGHT
PROJECT
A-Hotel, Chapel

ARCHITECT
RUI Architects, Engineers & Associates
Osaka, Japan

RENDERING SIZE
10" x 16" (25 cm x 41 cm)

MEDIA
Airbrush and watercolor

JAMES C. SMITH

THE STUDIO OF JAMES C. SMITH 700 SOUTH CLINTON STREET   CHICAGO, ILLINOIS 60607   312-987-0132 TEL   312-987-0099 FAX

Trained in the fine arts of painting and printmaking at Northwestern University, James C. Smith was influenced by the work of the early 20th-century surrealist movement. Moods, expressions, and visual animation are basic creative elements of his illustrations. After graduating with a Master of Fine Arts Degree, a seven-year interim career at a large architectural firm provided invaluable exposure to internationally renowned projects designed by master architects. Smith teaches advanced illustration techniques at Harrington Institute in Chicago, where he enjoys both instruction and professional practice.

The studio of James C. Smith has provided clients with dedication, expertise, service, and an unmatched work ethic for nineteen years. Smith forms a basic creative strategy with the client at the outset of a commission. He determines how the subject will be depicted based on considerations such as design criteria, project location, and the intended uses of the illustrations. A budget for the project is calculated using three factors: the complexity of the architecture, the media, and the schedule. Site visitation is extremely helpful in gaining impressions and determining the character of the project area. The studio's computer system provides the mechanical means for accurately plotting designs, layouts, and graphics. Typical commissions range from loose concept sketches to multiple airbrush presentation paintings.

ABOVE
PROJECT
440 North Wells Street
Chicago, Illinois
CLIENT
Urban Innovations
Chicago, Illinois
RENDERING SIZE
8" x 23" (20 cm x 58 cm)
MEDIA
Marker and pencil

LEFT
PROJECT
180 North LaSalle Street
Chicago, Illinois
CLIENT
Prime Group Realty Trust
Chicago, Illinois
RENDERING SIZE
12" x 15" (30 cm x 38 cm)
MEDIUM
Airbrush

OPPOSITE
PROJECT
1320 North Lake Shore Drive
Chicago, Illinois
CLIENT
Draper and Kramer, Inc.
Chicago, Illinois
RENDERING SIZE
28" x 17" (71 cm x 43 cm)
MEDIUM
Airbrush

PROJECT
Northbridge Development, Michigan Avenue
Chicago, Illinois

CLIENT
The John Buck Company
Chicago, Illinois

RENDERING SIZE
14" x 27" (36 cm x 69 cm)

MEDIUM
Airbrush

BELOW
PROJECT
Northbridge Development, 520 Mall
Chicago, Illinois

CLIENT
The John Buck Company
Chicago, Illinois

RENDERING SIZE
16" x 20" (41 cm x 51 cm)

MEDIUM
Airbrush

PROJECT
Northbridge Development, Disneyquest
Chicago, Illinois

CLIENT
The John Buck Company
Chicago, Illinois

RENDERING SIZE
14" x 40" (36 cm x 102 cm)

MEDIUM
Airbrush

BELOW
PROJECT
Northbridge Development, Grand Avenue
Chicago, Illinois

CLIENT
The John Buck Company
Chicago, Illinois

RENDERING SIZE
14" x 27" (36 cm x 69 cm)

MEDIUM
Airbrush

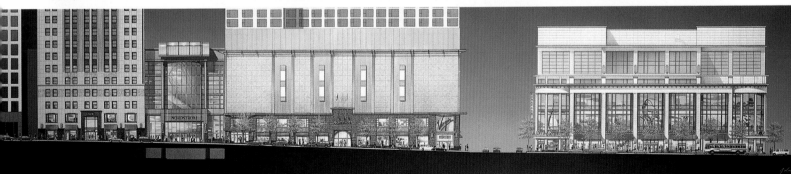

PROJECT
Northbridge Development, Michigan Avenue
Chicago, Illinois

CLIENT
The John Buck Company
Chicago, Illinois

RENDERING SIZE
14" x 40" (36 cm x 102 cm)

MEDIUM
Airbrush

LEFT
PROJECT
Wacker Tower
Chicago, Illinois

CLIENT
Markwell Properties
Chicago, Illinois

RENDERING SIZE
14" x 10" (36 cm x 25 cm)

MEDIUM
Airbrush

PROJECT
Wacker Tower
Chicago, Illinois

CLIENT
Markwell Properties
Chicago, Illinois

RENDERING SIZE
16" x 20" (41 cm x 51 cm)

MEDIA
Pen and ink, and colored pencil

PROJECT
Wacker Tower
Chicago, Illinois

CLIENT
Markwell Properties
Chicago, Illinois

RENDERING SIZES
9" x 11" (23 cm x 28 cm)

MEDIUM
Colored pencil on yellow trace

PROJECT
Ravenswood Park
Chicago, Illinois

CLIENT
Enterprise Development Company
Chicago, Illinois

RENDERING SIZE
20" x 23" (51 cm x 58 cm)

MEDIUM
Airbrush

BELOW
PROJECT
River North Commons
Chicago, Illinois

CLIENT
Enterprise Development Company
Chicago, Illinois

RENDERING SIZE
22" x 34" (56 cm x 86 cm)

MEDIUM
Airbrush

PROJECT
Prospect Heights Ice Arena
Prospect Heights, Illinois

ARCHITECT
Eckenhoff Saunders Architects
Chicago, Illinois

RENDERING SIZE
16" x 20" (41 cm x 51 cm)

BELOW
PROJECT
Notre Dame Stadium
South Bend, Indiana

CLIENT
University of Notre Dame

RENDERING SIZE
16" x 24" (41 cm x 61 cm)

MEDIUM
Airbrush

203

PROJECT
The Regal
Chicago, Illinois

CLIENT
Enterprise Development Company
Chicago, Illinois

RENDERING SIZE
18" x 32" (46 cm x 81 cm)

MEDIUM
Airbrush

DICK SNEARY

SNEARY ARCHITECTURAL ILLUSTRATION   9728 OVERHILL ROAD   KANSAS CITY, MISSOURI 64134   816-765-7841; 800-886-7117 TEL   816-763-0848 FAX

A registered architect and a member of the American Society of Architectural Perspectivists since 1989, Dick Sneary has been providing architectural illustrations to his clients for more than thirty years. Though he incorporates a variety of media, including ink, pencil, colored pencil, and pastel, Dick is primarily a watercolorist. He provides for his clients a wide range of techniques, ranging from small conceptual sketches to highly detailed finished renderings. Computer compatibility with AutoCAD and other CAD systems allows accurate perspectives and flexibility in choosing and altering views. His award-winning work has been jury-selected for nine consecutive Architecture in Perspective exhibitions. He has been featured in *The Art of Architectural Drawing, Architectural Rendering Techniques/A Color Reference, Drawing and Designing with Confidence, Art of Architectural Illustration 1, Architectural Design Collaborators 2 & 3,* and a variety of other publications. Sneary Architectural Illustration maintains an ongoing goal of achieving higher level of artistic excellence, while preserving its unique and distinctive style.

ABOVE
PROJECT
Kemper Arena Addition
Kansas City, Missouri

ARCHITECT
HNTB
Kansas City, Missouri

LEFT
PROJECT
University of Wisconsin
Madison, Wisconsin

ARCHITECT
HOK Sports Facilities Group
Kansas City, Missouri

PROJECT
Shaw Arboretum
Gray Summit, Missouri

ARCHITECT
Bohlin Cywinski Jackson
Philadelphia, Pennsylvania

RIGHT
PROJECT
Bartle Hall Convention Center
Kansas City, Missouri

ARCHITECT
BNIM Architects, Inc.
Kansas City, Missouri

BELOW
PROJECT
New Orleans Union Passenger Terminal
New Orleans, Louisiana

ARCHITECT
Billes/Manning Architects
New Orleans, Louisiana

PROJECT
Sports & Exposition Authority Arena
Camden, New Jersey

ARCHITECT
HOK Sports Facilities Group
Kansas City, Missouri

This piece won an Award of Excellence in
Architecture in Perspective 10.

PROJECT
Emory Law School, Gambrell Hall Expansion
Atlanta, Georgia

ARCHITECT
Heery International
Atlanta, Georgia

ABOVE LEFT
PROJECT
Carolinas Stadium Concourse

ARCHITECT
HOK Sports Facilities Group
Kansas City, Missouri

LEFT
PROJECT
Carolinas Stadium
Charlotte, North Carolina

ARCHITECT
HOK Sports Facilities Group
Kansas City, Missouri

This piece won the Formal Category Award
in Architecture in Perspective 12.

PROJECT
Baltimore Football Stadium
Baltimore, Maryland

ARCHITECT
HOK Sports Facilities Group
Kansas City, Missouri

PROJECT
Lakeside Nature Center
Kansas City, Missouri

ARCHITECT
International Architects Atelier
Kansas City, Missouri

BELOW
PROJECT
Branson Public Schools
Branson, Missouri

ARCHITECT
The Wischmeyer Architects, Inc.
Fayetteville, Arkansas

PROJECT
Travel Sketch

LEFT
PROJECT
Pacific Bell Park, O'Doul Bridge

ARCHITECT
HOK Sports Facilities Group
Kansas City, Missouri

PROJECT
New York Life Building Renovation
Kansas City, Missouri

ARCHITECT
Gassinger Walker Hardin Architects
Kansas City, Missouri

This piece won an Award of Excellence
at Architecture in Perspective 11.

RIGHT
PROJECT
Mall of Taiwan
Taiwan, China

ARCHITECT
Hellmuth, Obata + Kassabaum
Dallas, Texas

BELOW RIGHT
PROJECT
Glenview Naval Air Station
Redevelopment Project
Glenview, Illinois

ARCHITECT
Skidmore, Owings & Merrill Architects
Chicago, Illinois

AWARDS

*Formal Category Award, Architecture in
Perspective 12*

*Award of Excellence, Architecture in Perspective
4, 5, 6, 7, 9, 10, and 11*

*Jack O. Hedrich Juror's Award, Architecture in
Perspective 8*

PARTIAL CLIENT LIST

Hellmuth, Obata + Kassabaum, Dallas, Texas

*HOK Sports Facilities Group, Kansas City,
Missouri*

*Skidmore, Owings, and Merrill Architects,
Chicago, Illinois*

*Bohlin Cywinski Jackson, Philadelphia,
Pennsylvania*

HKS Inc., Dallas, Texas

Dale Associates Architects, Jackson, Mississippi

*Heinlein + Schrock Architecture,
Kansas City, Missouri*

ZBM Partners Architects, Omaha, Nebraska

BNIM Architects Inc., Kansas City, Missouri

Shopping Center, Uberaba, Brazil

THE BRAZIL-PORTUGAL CONNECTION

BY ANGELO DeCASTRO

Architectural rendering has evolved into an international profession. Even renderers who do little or no traveling sometimes find themselves drawing buildings in distant locations with strange and unknown climates and cultures. An understanding of these climates and cultures can often make the difference between a successful and an unsuccessful drawing.

Ten years ago, I emigrated from Brazil to Portugal, from a country that had very few professional renderers to one that had none at all. Because Portugal had recently joined the European Community, there was a strong need to create infrastructure to modernize the country. Real estate was booming, and the market was favorable for architects, my first clients in Europe.

On arriving in Europe, I noticed the differences in cultural climate and tastes between the two continents. Despite some common languages and certain similarities of climate, Europeans have very different ideas about how they want their environment depicted than South Americans do.

Brazil, where I began my career, is a tropical country. Brazilians like intense colors with strong contrast. Vegetation is abundant, so many different tones of green are used. The sea and the sky are always blue. Even though Brazil is a huge "continental country" and each of its five regions has contrasting vegetation, climate, culture, and ethnicity, the sun always prevails.

My illustration experience was mostly concentrated in Brazil's southeast, where the developments in and the demands of illustration are greater. In the beginning, most of my clients were architects who preferred the detail and precision of ink line drawing. During the real estate boom of the '70s, the construction of many apartment buildings, huge condos, hotels, and vacation resorts brought a change of techniques: Real-estate developers, property advisors, and advertisers were calling for illustrations in airbrush, which enabled a sophisticated but informal and cheerful atmosphere. Today, drawings are mostly used for advertising purposes.

This differs from rendering in some other South American countries I have had the opportunity to observe. In Chile and Argentina, for instance, there is a strong European influence in both architecture and illustration. The use of colored pencil and watercolor is predominant, creating soft illustrations with little contrast.

When I arrived in Europe, I had a great deal of experience—all of it South American. I was aware that the climate in Europe was different: The seasons are well defined—the summer is strong and sunny, the winter gray and wet, the spring and fall colorful with blue skies most of the time. But I still found the light to be strong and intense. Clients, however, always requested that I use soft tones with little contrast, such as grays, beiges, and pinks. With time, I realized that this was a cultural issue. Portugal had been cut off from other European countries for many years due to a dictatorial political system. People used dark and discrete colors. Besides, gray is a European color!

To adapt their work to the reality of the client, illlustrators need to understand local political and cultural issues. After becoming part of the European market, Portugal has gradually become much more open to new ideas. Now, each region has developed its own characteristics and demands. Porto, located in the north of Portugal, is colder and the architecture, purist and more formal. There is a strong use of white, gray, brick red, and ocher. In the country's center and capital, Lisbon, the weather is mixed, and the architecture more informal and diverse, ranging from the high-tech to the traditional Portuguese style. International influences in Lisbon have promoted the use of different techniques, and most clients are ready to try new ideas.

In the Algarve, in the south of the country, it is sunny and hot most of the time, and vacation resorts predominate. Despite being on the Atlantic Ocean, there is a strong Mediterranean and North African influence. The characteristic vegetation of pine trees, bougainvillea, and cacti brings more colorful results.

Other European countries seem also to have national tastes when it comes to rendering. In Germany, where I have been working with architects and real estate developers, the modern architecture seems to me to be very technical and formal. There is strong use of metal, glass, and granite. Even with materials such as brick or wood, the colors tend to be dark. From the basic perspective concept to the final artwork, precision and attention to detail are very important to German clients. The entourage, cars, trees, and figures are very carefully studied. The most commonly used media are airbrush and computer rendering, using sophisticated software for high quality results.

I have observed that other European countries show preferences that might be said to reflect a national style. In the Netherlands, for example, illustrators produce excellent effects with shady tones of sunset and somber colors. Although the weather in England is wet and gray most of the time, illustrators there represent architecture in a more informal way with beautiful watercolors in light tones and with little contrast. French artists, on the other hand, are very concerned with entourage, especially the gardens and the vegetation. Drawings are romantic and charming, bright and yet opaque. Tempera is predominant.

My experience in North America is limited, but through books and brochures, I have observed that there is a great variety of styles and a wide use of different techniques there. Moreover, there is great artistic freedom due to the wealthy and extensive market. Renderings with the aid of computer software are widely used for wireframes or final artwork, providing illustrators with accurate and sometimes quick results. However, traditional techniques such as watercolor, colored pencil, ink line, tempera, and airbrush for sketches or detailed renderings are still greatly appreciated and highly respected.

Moving across continents, it's become obvious to me that it is important to consider the different social, cultural, geographical, and even historical aspects of the location you are rendering as well as the requirements of a particular client. Although illustrations are and will always be a fascinating means of communication, they have to represent the reality of each country, each project, and each client. Great architectural projects usually turn into excellent illustrations! This is the same everywhere in the world.

Cimpor Tower, Maputo, Mozambique

Office Building, Lisbon, Portugal

Spree Forum, Berlin, Germany

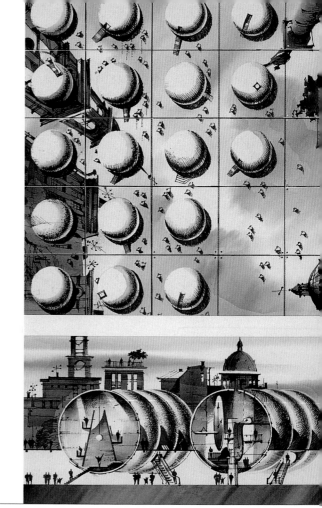

SERGEI E. TCHOBAN

NPS UND PARTNER   ROSENTHALER STR. 40-41   HACKESCHE HÖFE, HOF 2   10178 BERLIN, GERMANY

The drawings of Sergei E. Tchoban express sensational and paradoxical space and imagery through various and unique technical approaches. The influence of the traditional Russian constructivists or an impression of the mysterious arcades from Piranesi or Guardi may linger in an illustration, but Tchoban's modern style with its dynamic, unfinished lines never gives the impression of being incomplete. Watercolor, sepia ink, and pen are used in most of the artist's works. This approach enables Tchoban to connect conventional and established media in a spectacular and astonishing fashion that produces powerful, but subtle, insights throughout the drawing process. Tchoban particularly enjoys creating renderings for buildings that can be illustrated diversely through his sepia-watercolor technique. The world of fantastical architectural illusion plays an important part in the artist's realization of "real" projects, in which distinct details of remarkable, "unreal" images can now and then be discovered.

PROJECT
Spaces for Art Exhibition Rooms
Free composition
Hamburg, Germany

RENDERING SIZE
24" x 18" (61 cm x 46 cm)

MEDIA
Watercolor, pen, and sepia ink

PROJECT
Windows and Stairs
Free composition
Hamburg, Germany

RENDERING SIZE
18" x 18" (46 cm x 46 cm)

MEDIA
Watercolor, pen, and sepia ink

213

PROJECT
Watergames
Free composition
Hamburg, Germany

RENDERING SIZE
18" x 18" (46 cm x 46 cm)

MEDIA
Watercolor, pen, and sepia ink

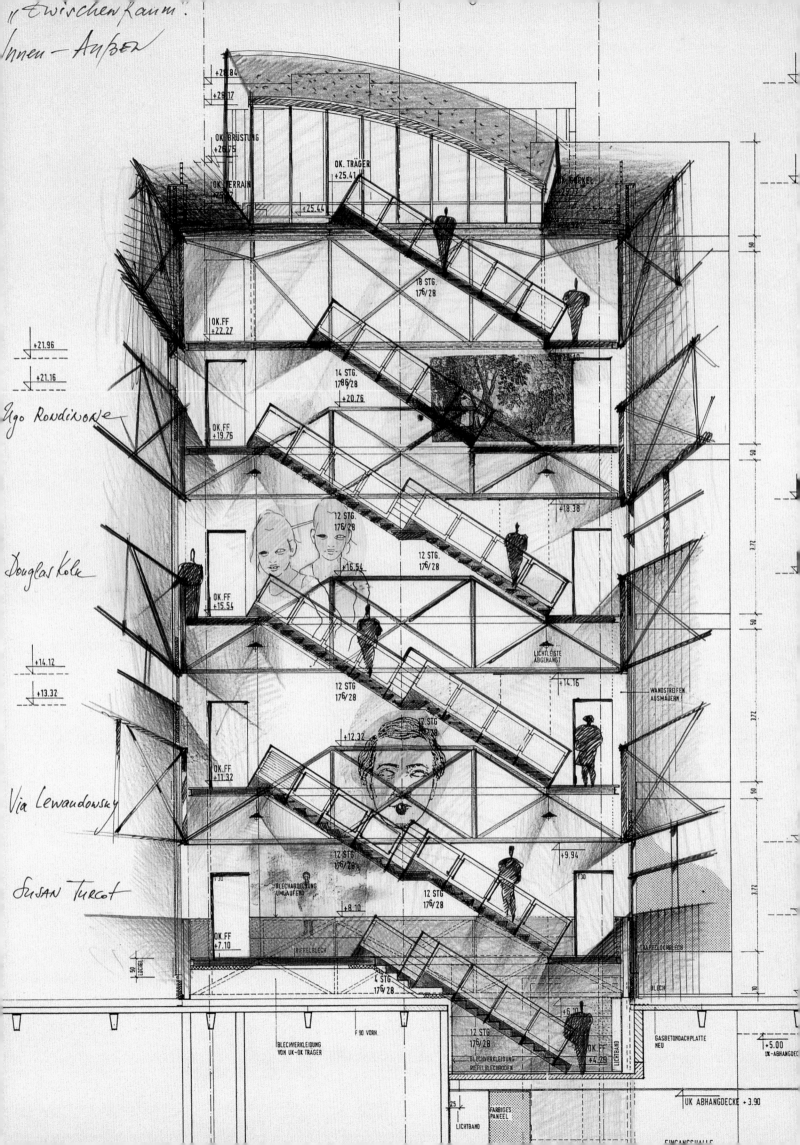

"Zwischenraum":
Innen – Außen

Ugo Rondinone

Douglas Kolk

Via Lewandowsky

Susan Turcot

OPPOSITE

PROJECT
Java-Tower, Stairs
Free composition
Hamburg, Germany

ARCHITECTS
Nietz Prasch Sigl
Tchoban Voss
Hamburg, Germany

CLIENT
Wilhelm Pabel
GmbH & Co. KG

RENDERING SIZE
17" x 28" (43 cm x 71 cm)

MEDIA
Prismacolor and pencil

RIGHT

PROJECT
Venice Dream
Free composition
Hamburg, Germany

RENDERING SIZE
14" x 20" (36 cm x 51 cm)

MEDIA
Watercolor, pen, and sepia ink

BELOW

PROJECT
Bridges
Free composition
Hamburg, Germany

RENDERING SIZE
13" x 24" (33 cm x 61 cm)

MEDIA
Watercolor, pen, and sepia ink

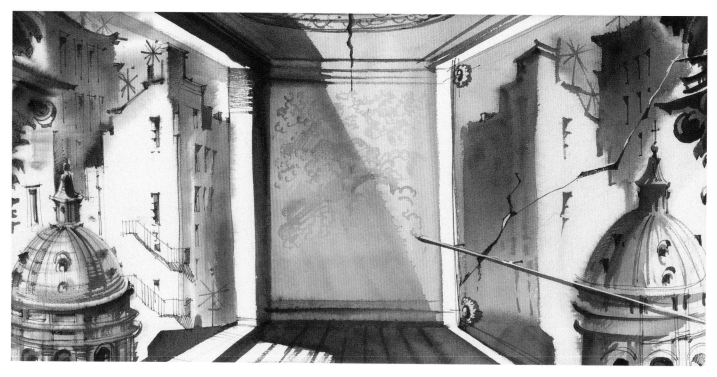

ABOVE
PROJECT
Private Residence

RENDERING SIZE
9" x 20" (23 cm x 50 cm)

MEDIA
Watercolor and sepia ink

OPPOSITE
PROJECT
The Simple Forms

RENDERING SIZE
16" x 24" (41 cm x 61 cm)

MEDIA
Watercolor and sepia ink

BELOW
PROJECT
Ponte Vecchio

RENDERING SIZE
14" x 22" (36 cm x 56 cm)

MEDIA
Watercolor and sepia ink

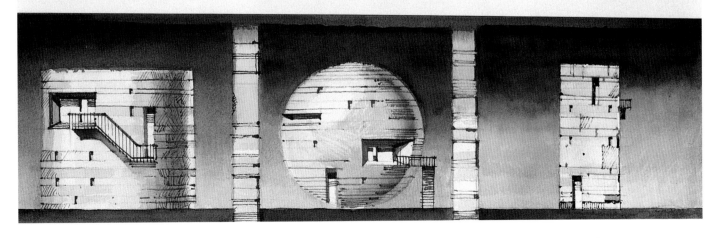

WILLEM VAN DEN HOED

1000 HUIZEN LANGE GEER 44   2611 PW DELFT   THE NETHERLANDS   31-15-213-3382 TEL   31-15-212-0448 FAX

During the last two years, the work done at 1000 Huizen in Delft has shifted from illustration to architectural design. More and more, the drawings created are original design drawings instead of illustrations of the ideas of clients. Willem van den Hoed is using his ten years of illustration experience to realize and build his own visions.

Most illustrations included on these pages were created, in part, with the help of computers. Even small hand-drawn sketches can be scanned and improved digitally. An original drawing may no longer exist. The drawings are sometimes manipulated during the project and exist in several stages as files on a CD-ROM. From there, they can be e-mailed to clients, or they can be included in desktop publishing publications. They can even be sent to magazines and printers without expensive photography and lithography.

The drawings themselves can be scanned photographs, digitally manipulated hand-drawn sketches, or computer renderings. Computer renderings, in turn, can be created from scanned photographs, CAD drawings, or even hand-drawn sketches. The availability of inexpensive, fast computers opens up many graphical possibilities for the illustrator and architect. The office of Willem van den Hoed is going through an exciting digital revolution.

THIS PAGE AND OPPOSITE
PROJECT
European Housing Competition
Hirvensalo Island (near Turku, Finland)
ARCHITECT
02901EUROPE
RENDERING SIZE
3,000 x 4,000 pixels
MEDIUM
Computer-generated

BD 591

044 PIHLAJANIEMI

219

SITE

PROJECT
Primary School and Schoolyard
Utrecht, the Netherlands

ARCHITECT
Willem van den Hoed

MEDIA
Fineliner, marker, and colored pencil on paper
(digitally retouched)

RIGHT
PROJECT
Transformer Station on Dataport
Rotterdam, the Netherlands

ARCHITECT
Willem van den Hoed in collaboration
with Le Gué Beheer

MEDIA
Fineliner, marker, and colored pencil on paper
(digitally retouched)

BELOW LEFT AND RIGHT
PROJECT
Office Building for Topos Architecten
Waddinxveen, the Netherlands

ARCHITECT
Willem van den Hoed

MEDIA
Fineliner, marker, and colored pencil on paper
(digitally retouched)

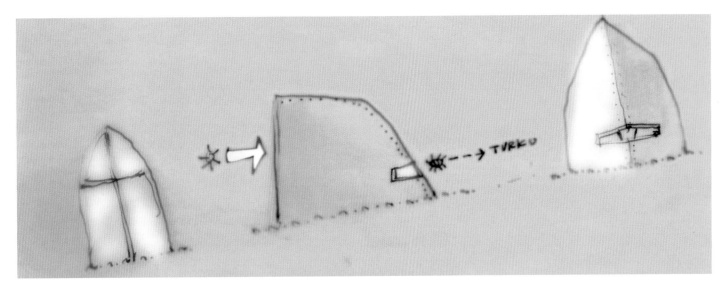

PROJECT
European Housing Competition
Hirvensalo Island (near Turku, Finland)

ARCHITECT
02901EUROPE

MEDIUM
Fineliner on paper (digitally retouched)

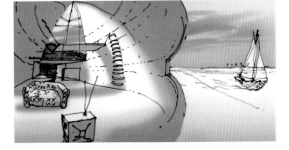

PROJECT
de Twijn School
The Hague, the Netherlands

ARCHITECT
Willem van den Hoed

MEDIA
Fineliner, marker, and color pencil on paper

PROJECT
Jephta Plein Housing
Haarlem, the Netherlands

ARCHITECT
Willem van den Hoed

MEDIA
Fineliner, marker, and colored pencil on paper

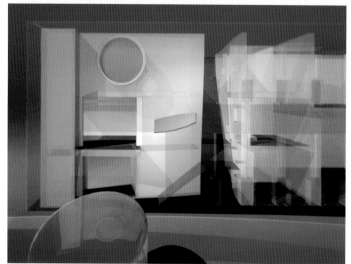

PROJECT
Primary School
Utrecht, the Netherlands

ARCHITECT
Willem van den Hoed

MEDIUM
Computer-generated

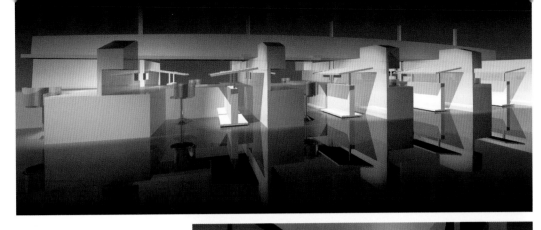

PROJECT
Office building for Topos Architecten
Waddinxveen, the Netherlands

ARCHITECT
Willem van den Hoed

MEDIUM
Computer-generated

ANDREW S.K. WEE

AW DESIGN DELINEATION   453 UPPER EAST COAST ROAD   #03-03 THE SUMMIT   SINGAPORE 466501   SINGAPORE   +65-442-3115 TEL
+65-244-9250 FAX   EMAIL AW_DESIGN@PACIFIC.NET.SG

Andrew Wee is the founder and principal of AW Design Delineation, a studio that provides extensive services from perspective rendering to design consultancy. He has more than ten years' experience working as the chief designer of several established architectural firms in Singapore. He is also the founding partner of an architectural firm, in which he was the head of design and presentation. Andrew received his Bachelor of Architecture Degree from the University of Oklahoma

His passion for drawing has compelled him to explore many different media and rendering techniques over the years. Today, he has become one of the most versatile illustrators in his region. His works have been honored with an Award of Excellence by the American Society of Architectural Perspectivists (ASAP) in Architecture in Perspective competitions and exhibitions. His design skill and professional expertise in diverse rendering styles make him highly sought-after by architectural firms, developers, and marketing agencies. Architects benefit greatly from his on-site consultancy services—these often involve direct design participation in design charrettes, providing design ideas and imagery from atmospheric sketches to finished renderings.

ABOVE
PROJECT
Design & Build competition for Housing
Development Board
Singapore
ARCHITECT
K. C. Kan Architects
RENDERING SIZE
18" x 14" (46 cm x 36 cm)
MEDIA
Marker and colored pencil

BELOW
PROJECT
Willow Hill Condominium
Singapore
ARCHITECT
Wimberly Allison Tong & Goo
RENDERING SIZE
26" x 18" (66 cm x 46 cm)
MEDIUM
Colored pencil on paper

ABOVE
PROJECT
Design & Build competition for
Housing Development Board
Singapore

ARCHITECT
K. C. Kan Architects

RENDERING SIZE
16" x 9" (41 cm x 23 cm)

MEDIUM
Marker and colored pencil on paper

RIGHT
PROJECT
Mixed-use Development
Penang, Malaysia

ARCHITECT
Wimberly Allison Tong & Goo

RENDERING SIZE
14" x 8" (36 cm x 20 cm), top;
14" x 9" (36 cm x 23 cm), middle;
14" x 10" (36 cm x 25 cm), bottom

MEDIA
Marker and colored pencil

PROJECT
Waterfront commercial
development
Da Lien, China

ARCHITECT
Wimberly Allison Tong & Goo

RENDERING SIZE
22" x 18" (56 cm x 46 cm)

MEDIUM
Gouache on illustration board

LEFT
PROJECT
Convention Centre
Da Lien, China
ARCHITECT
Wimberly Allison Tong & Goo
RENDERING SIZE
24" x 14" (61 cm x 36 cm)
MEDIUM
Gouache on illustration board

BELOW RIGHT
PROJECT
Mixed use development
Da Lien, China
ARCHITECT
Wimberly Allison Tong & Goo
RENDERING SIZE
20" x 12" (51 cm x 30 cm)
MEDIUM
Gouache on illustration board

226

ABOVE LEFT
PROJECT
Golf Club
Kwang Zhou, China
ARCHITECT
Andrew Wee/AW Design Delineation
RENDERING SIZE
20" x 12" (51 cm x 30 cm)
MEDIUM
Gouache on illustration board

LEFT
PROJECT
Residential development
Cairnhill, Singapore
ARCHITECT
Andrew S. K. Wee
RENDERING SIZE
18" x 12" (46 cm x 30 cm)
MEDIUM
Gouache on illustration board

BELOW
PROJECT
Mixed use development
China Square, Singapore
ARCHITECT
ADDP Architects
RENDERING SIZE
22" x 16" (56 cm x 41 cm)
MEDIUM
Gouache on illustration board

BELOW
PROJECT
Airport design proposal
ARCHITECT
Airport Development Division, PWD
RENDERING SIZE
22" x 16" (56 cm x 41 cm)
MEDIUM
Gouache on illustration board

RIGHT
PROJECT
Golf Lodge Hotel
Da Lien, China
ARCHITECT
Wimberly Allison Tong & Goo
RENDERING SIZE
20" x 14" (51 cm x 36 cm)
MEDIUM
Gouache on illustration board

227

ABOVE RIGHT
PROJECT
Condominium development
Bishan, Singapore
ARCHITECT
Andrew S. K. Wee (as design partner of Axis
Architects/Planners)
RENDERING SIZE
18" x 13" (46 cm x 33 cm)
MEDIUM
Gouache on illustration board

BELOW
PROJECT
Industrial Project
Tuas, Singapore
ARCHITECT
K. C. Kan Architects
RENDERING SIZE
16" x 14" (41 cm x 36 cm)
MEDIUM
Mixed media

RIGHT
PROJECT
Commercial Project
China Square, Singapore
ARCHITECT
ADDP Architects
RENDERING SIZE
24" x 16" (61 cm x 41 cm)
MEDIUM
Mixed media

PROJECT
Airport design proposal
ARCHITECT
Airport Development Division, PWD
RENDERING SIZE
18" x 12" (46 cm x 30 cm)
MEDIUM
Gouache on illustration board

PROJECT
Master Plan for reclamation project
Tanjong Tokong, Penang, Malaysia

ARCHITECT
Wimberly Allison Tong & Goo Architects

RENDERING SIZE
14" x 8" (36 cm x 20 cm)

MEDIUM
Colored pencil on paper

228

LEFT

PROJECT
Master Plan for reclamation project
Tanjong Tokong, Penang, Malaysia

ARCHITECT
Wimberly Allison Tong & Goo

RENDERING SIZE
14" x 10" (36 cm x 25 cm)

MEDIUM
Marker and colored pencil on paper

BELOW LEFT

PROJECT
Waterfront condominium
Tanjong Tokong, Penang, Malaysia

ARCHITECT
Wimberly Allison Tong & Goo

RENDERING SIZE
12" x 10" (30 cm x 25 cm)

MEDIUM
Marker and colored pencil on paper

BELOW RIGHT

PROJECT
Entertainment Complex
Tanjong Tokong, Penang, Malaysia

ARCHITECT
Wimberly Allison Tong & Goo

RENDERING SIZE
20" x 18" (51 cm x 19 cm)

MEDIUM
Gouache on illustration board

This piece won the Award of Excellence in
Architecture in Perspective 13

ABOVE AND RIGHT
PROJECT
Robertson Quay Development

ARCHITECT
Andrew S. K. Wee

RENDERING SIZE
9" x 6" (23 cm x 15 cm)

MEDIUM
Pen and ink

229

PROJECT
Yin Residence

ARCHITECT
Andrew S. K. Wee

RENDERING SIZE
10" x 6" (25 cm x 15 cm)

MEDIUM
Pen and ink

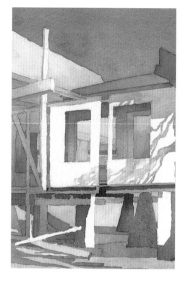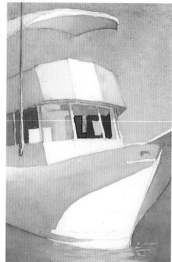

CURTIS JAMES WOODHOUSE

3903 LOQUAT AVENUE   COCONUT GROVE, FLORIDA 33133   305-476-8098 TEL   305-476-8096

Curtis Woodhouse is a Miami-based architect and illustrator who feels that his design and planning experience is essential when working with clients and producing successful illustration. While favoring watercolor, Woodhouse works with a variety of media at several scales and degrees of refinement. Much of Woodhouse's work involves direct design collaboration, and he has participated in many charrettes and on-site workshops.

ABOVE
PROJECT
Field Studies
Marathon, Florida

BELOW
PROJECT
American Bankers Insurance Group
Miami, Florida
ARCHITECT
Spillis, Candela & Partners, Inc.

PROJECT
Sasson Hotel Tower

ARCHITECT
Schapiro Associates

PROJECT
Dolphin Mall
Miami, Florida

ARCHITECT
Beame Architectural Partnership

WOOD MANSION"
gh Limit Tables

OVENTURE CASINO SOUNDSTAGE"
Action: Jurassic Park

SCI-FI CASINO SOUNDSTAGE"
Superheroes: Batman

ABOVE
PROJECT
Planet Hollywood Casino
Las Vegas, Nevada

ARCHITECT
Rockwell Architecture

BELOW
PROJECT
VisionLand Outlet Center
Charlotte, North Carolina

ARCHITECT
Adams Hennon Architects

PROJECT
Flatiron Crossing Mall
Boulder, Colorado
ARCHITECT
Callison Architecture, Inc.

PROJECT
Michael Jordan's Steakhouse
New York, New York
ARCHITECT
Rockwell Architecture

PROJECT
Pusan Harbor
Pusan, South Korea
ARCHITECT
Sasaki Associates, Inc.
(collaboration with Thomas Schaller)

PROJECT
Savannah Courthouse
Savannah, Georgia
ARCHITECT
Robert A. M. Stern Architects

PROJECT
Keewaydin Island
Naples, Florida
ARCHITECT
Architectural Design Group, Inc.

DAVID XIAOPING XU

3050 PHARMACY AVE., #808   TORONTO, ONTARIO M1W 2N7 CANADA   416-492-3260 TEL

David Xiaoping Xu has been dedicated to architectural illustration and interior design for eight years. He not only is specialized in realistic airbrushed images with fine details and material textures, but also is proficient in other techniques and media, such as watercolor, pen and ink, and colored pencil. He works closely with several large architectural and interior design firms, advertising agencies, and developers throughout China. He is now working in Toronto, Canada, in his profession.

He is a member of both The American Society of Architectural Perspectivists and of China Interior Designers Association. Xiaoping received an Award of Excellence in Architecture in Perspective 12.

ABOVE
PROJECT
JITIC Office Building
Nanjing, China
ARCHITECT
Zhong Da Architecture Design Co.
Nanjing, China
RENDERING SIZE
30" x 20.5" (76 cm x 52 cm)
MEDIA
Gouache and airbrush

PROJECT
Teaching and Researching Building
Wuhan, China
ARCHITECT
Zhong Da Architecture Design Co.
Nanjing, China
RENDERING SIZE
34.5" x 23" (88 cm x 58 cm)
MEDIA
Gouache and airbrush

PROJECT
Jiangsu Opera House
Nanjing, China

ARCHITECT
Zhong Da Architecture Design Co.
Nanjing, China

RENDERING SIZE
34.5" x 23" (88 cm x 58 cm)

MEDIA
Gouache and airbrush

PROJECT
Zhangjiagang Hotel
Zhangjiagang, China

ARCHITECT
W2 Architecture & Interior Design
Nanjing, China

RENDERING SIZE
30" x 20.5" (76 cm x 52 cm)

MEDIA
Gouache and airbrush

PROJECT
Lake Shore Hotel
Wuxi, China

ARCHITECT
Zhong Da Architecture Design Co.
Nanjing, China

RENDERING SIZE
34.5" x 23" (88 cm x 58 cm)

MEDIA
Gouache and airbrush

RIGHT
PROJECT
Yanfu Hotel, Presidential Suite
Yancheng, China

CLIENT
N. J. Decoration Engineering Company
Nanjing, China

RENDERING SIZE
30" x 20.5" (76 cm x 52 cm)

MEDIUM
Gouache and airbrush

238

PROJECT
The Eastern Suburbs Guest House
Nanjing, China

ARCHITECT
W2 Architecture & Interior Design
Nanjing, China

RENDERING SIZE
20.5" x 14.5" (52 cm x 37 cm)

MEDIA
Gouache, airbrush, and colored pencil

ABOVE RIGHT
PROJECT
Assembly Hall
Yangzhou, China

CLIENT
N. J . Decoration Engineering Company
Nanjing, China

RENDERING SIZE
30" x 20.5" (76 cm x 52 cm)

MEDIA
Gouache, airbrush, and colored pencil

RIGHT
PROJECT
Jianda Hotel, Dining Hall,
Nanjing, China

ARCHITECT
Drawingway Design Company. Ltd.
Nanjing, China

CLIENT
Crown Decoration Engineering Company, Ltd.
Nanjing, China

RENDERING SIZE
26.875" x 16.5 (68 cm x 42 cm)

MEDIA
Gouache, airbrush, and colored pencil

239

PROJECT
Jianda Hotel, Lobby
Nanjing, China

ARCHITECT
Drawingway Design Company, Ltd.
Nanjing, China

CLIENT
Crown Decoration Engineering Company, Ltd.
Nanjing, China

RENDERING SIZE
26.875" x 16.5 (68 cm x 42 cm)

MEDIA
Gouache, airbrush, and colored pencil

PROJECT
Jianda Hotel, Restaurant
Nanjing, China

ARCHITECT
Drawingway Design Company, Ltd.
Nanjing, China

CLIENT
Crown Decoration Engineering Company, Ltd.
Nanjing, China

RENDERING SIZE
26.875" x 16.5 (68 cm x 42 cm)

MEDIA
Gouache, airbrush, and colored pencil

PROJECT
New Wave Plaza
Nanjing, China

ARCHITECT
Zhong Da Architecture Design Co.
Nanjing, China

RENDERING SIZE
30" x 20.5" (76 cm x 52 cm)

MEDIA
Gouache and airbrush

PROJECT
Lobby, Jianye District
Governmental Office Building
Nanjing, China

ARCHITECT
Drawingway Design Company, Ltd.
Nanjing, China

CLIENT
Crown Decoration Engineering Company, Ltd.

RENDERING SIZE
30" x 20.5" (76 cm x 52 cm)

MEDIA
Gouache and airbrush

PROJECT
The Eastern Suburbs Guest House,
Presidential Suite
Nanjing, China

ARCHITECT
W2 Architecture & Interior Design
Nanjing, China

RENDERING SIZE
20.5" x 14.5" (52 cm x 37 cm)

MEDIA
Gouache, airbrush, and colored pencil

PROJECT
Science and Technology Building,
Nanjing University
Nanjing, China

ARCHITECT
The Institute of Architecture Design & Research
Southeast University
Nanjing, China

RENDERING SIZE
30" x 20.5" (76 cm x 52 cm)

MEDIA
Gouache and airbrush

PROJECT
Airport Highway Inspection Centre, Lobby
Nanjing, China

ARCHITECT
W2 Architecture & Interior Design
Nanjing, China

RENDERING SIZE
30" x 20.5" (76 cm x 52 cm)

MEDIA
Gouache, airbrush, and colored pencil

MASAAKI YAMADA

NIKKEN SEKKEI LTD. 2-1-3 KORAKU BUNKYO-KU, TOKYO 112-8565 JAPAN 03-3813-3361 TEL 03-3817-0755 FAX
yamadam@nikken.co.jp

Masaaki Yamada is an architectural illustrator currently based in Tokyo as a member of the presentation group at Nikken Sekkei, Japan's largest architectural and engineering firm. For ten years, Yamada lived in Los Angeles, where he learned a variety of rendering and illustration techniques. For the last five years, he has been refining his presentation skills on the broad range of Nikken Sekkei projects that benefit from his ability to translate imagination into image.

Most of his work forms an integral part of competition submissions; Yamada creates early stage image sketches for project proposals and for direct presentation to clients. He chooses an illustration medium that will harmonize with the overall presentation. Media Yamada favors include pen and ink, watercolor, pastel, and colored pencil.

Masaaki Yamada personally strives to impart a lifelike quality of place, people, and landscape in his images. He works closely with the design team to ensure that his illustrations fully and powerfully express the ideas that must be brought into focus, often in a very short period of time. Two of Yamada's illustrations have been recognized with Awards of Excellence from the ASAP's 12th and 13th Architecture in Perspective competitions.

PROJECT
Project P Proposal
Yaesu, Tokyo, Japan
ARCHITECT
Nikken Sekkei
RENDERING SIZE
11" x 13" (28 cm x 33 cm)
MEDIA
Watercolor and colored pencil

PROJECT
Shiodome Redevelopment Project
Tokyo, Japan

ARCHITECT
Nikken Sekkei

RENDERING SIZE
10" x 16" (25 cm x 41 cm)

MEDIUM
Watercolor

RIGHT
PROJECT
Shiodome Redevelopment Project
Tokyo, Japan

ARCHITECT
Nikken Sekkei

RENDERING SIZE
12" x 16" (30 cm x 41 cm)

MEDIA
Pen and ink with watercolor

BELOW RIGHT
PROJECT
Project S Proposal
Tokyo, Japan

ARCHITECT
Nikken Sekkei

RENDERING SIZE
12" x 21" (30 cm x 53 cm)

MEDIA
Watercolor and colored pencil

PROJECT
Yamagata Station,
West Gate Building Competition
Yamagata, Japan

ARCHITECT
Nikken Sekkei

RENDERING SIZE
20" x 16" (51 cm x 41 cm)

MEDIUM
Watercolor

ABOVE LEFT
PROJECT
Okawabata Super Stadium Proposal
Tokyo, Japan
ARCHITECT
Nikken Sekkei
RENDERING SIZE
7" x 13" (18 cm x 33 cm)
MEDIUM
Watercolor

LEFT
PROJECT
Saitama Municipal and
Government Office Building
Saitama, Japan
ARCHITECT
Nikken Sekkei
RENDERING SIZE
13" x 15" (33 cm x 38 cm)
MEDIA
Pen and ink with watercolor

BELOW LEFT
PROJECT
Labor Experience Plaza
Keihanna Area, Japan
ARCHITECT
Nikken Sekkei
RENDERING SIZE
10" x 12" (25 cm x 30 cm)
MEDIA
Watercolor and colored pencil

PROJECT
Tom Ling Son Road Mixed
Development Competition
Singapore

ARCHITECT
Nikken Sekkei

RENDERING SIZE
12" x 25" (30 cm x 64 cm)

MEDIUM
Watercolor

BELOW
PROJECT
Shanghai National Museum Competition
Shanghai, China

ARCHITECT
Nikken Sekkei

RENDERING SIZE
15" x 26" (38 cm x 66 cm)

MEDIA
Watercolor and colored pencil

PROJECT
Shanghai Office Building Competition
Shanghai, China

ARCHITECT
Nikken Sekkei

RENDERING SIZE
9" x 13" (23 cm x 33 cm)

MEDIUM
Watercolor

LEFT
PROJECT
Shanghai National Opera House Competition
Shanghai, China

ARCHITECT
Nikken Sekkei

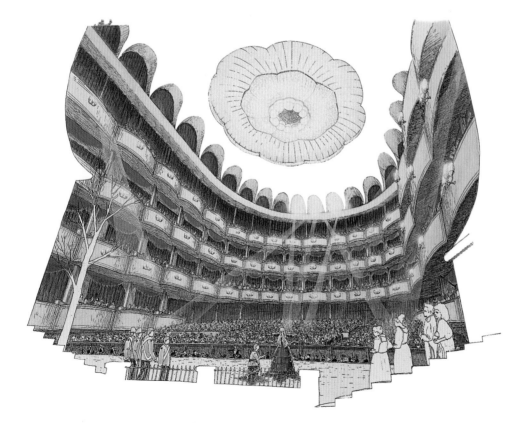

PROJECT
Song-Do Newtown, Conceptual Master Plan
Song-Do, South Korea

ARCHITECT
Nikken Sekkei

RENDERING SIZE
7" x 12" (18 cm x 30 cm)

MEDIA
Pen, colored pencil, and pastel

PROJECT
Song-Do Newtown, Conceptual Master Plan
Song-Do, South Korea

ARCHITECT
Nikken Sekkei

RENDERING SIZE
5" x 11" (13 cm x 28 cm)

MEDIA
Pen, colored pencil, and pastel

PROJECT
Song-Do Newtown, Conceptual Master Plan
Song-Do, South Korea

ARCHITECT
Nikken Sekkei

RENDERING SIZE
6" x 10" (15 cm x 25 cm)

MEDIA
Pen, colored pencil, and pastel

247

PROJECT
Saitama Arena
Saitama, Japan

ARCHITECT
Nikken Sekkei

RENDERING SIZE
7" x 13" (18 cm x 33 cm)

MEDIA
Pen, colored pencil, and pastel

PROJECT
Saitama Arena
Saitama, Japan

ARCHITECT
Nikken Sekkei

RENDERING SIZE
9" x 12" (23 cm x 30 cm)

MEDIA
Pen, colored pencil, and pastel

TAMOTSU YAMAMOTO

15 SLEEPER STREET   BOSTON, MASSACHUSETTS 02210   617-542-1021 TEL   617-451-0271 FAX   DADA13@AOL.COM

Tamotsu Yamamoto is a skilled artist whose services include watercolor, gouache, pen and ink, airbrush, colored pencil, and other drawing media. Adept at working with architects, developers, and interior designers in the early stages of design conceptualization, Yamamoto creates quick sketches in any medium through final presentation renderings. He has been working in the Boston area since 1973, serving a worldwide clientele.

Yamamoto has taught perspective theory, rendering, and design communication technique since 1979 at colleges in the Boston area, and his works have been exhibited not only throughout the United States but in Europe and Southeast Asia. He is past president of the American Society of Architectural Perspectivists, and an honorary member of the Japan Architectural Renderers Association.

ABOVE
ARCHITECT
Carlson Associates
Framingham, Massachusetts
RENDERING SIZE
13" x 18" (33 cm x 46 cm)
MEDIUM
Watercolor

BELOW
PROJECT
Omaha Botanical Garden Proposal
Omaha, Nebraska
ARCHITECT
Zen Associates, Inc.
Sudbury, Massachusetts
RENDERING SIZE
16" x 34" (41 cm x 86 cm)
MEDIUM
Watercolor

PROJECT
Desert Storm Memorial Competition
Kuwait City, Kuwait

ARCHITECT
HDS/Hans D. Strauch & Associates, Inc.
Boston, Massachusetts

RENDERING SIZE
22" x 30"(56 cm x 76 cm)

MEDIUM
Watercolor

RIGHT
PROJECT
Massachusetts College of Art
Boston, Massachusetts

RENDERING SIZE
12.25" x 17.5" (31 cm x 44 cm)

MEDIA
Watercolor and tempera

This sample shows a quick sketch.

PROJECT
PerSeptive Biosystems, Corporate Headquarters
Framingham, Massachusetts

ARCHITECT
Clifford/Hoffman Associates
Boston, Massachusetts

RENDERING SIZE
8.5" x 10.5" (22 cm x 27 cm)

MEDIUM
Watercolor

BELOW
PROJECT
Competition winning project in China

ARCHITECT
Skidmore, Owings & Merrill Architects
Chicago, Illinois

RENDERING SIZE
11" x 17" (28 cm x 43 cm)

MEDIUM
Conceptual sketch with colored pencil

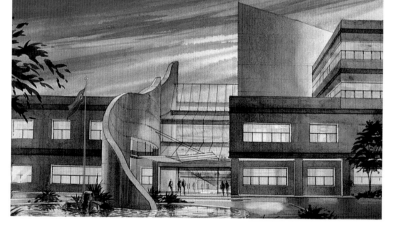

PROJECT
Asmara Medical Center
Asmara, Eritrea, Africa

ARCHITECT
DTS Shaw Associates, Inc.
Boston, Massachusetts

RENDERING SIZE
13" x 21" (33 cm x 53 cm)

MEDIUM
Watercolor

This rendering depicts an aerial view of the
Center.

PROJECT
Asmara Medical Center
Asmara, Eritrea, Africa

ARCHITECT
DTS Shaw Associates, Inc.
Boston, Massachusetts

RENDERING SIZE
13" x 21" (33 cm x 53 cm)

MEDIUM
Watercolor

This rendering depicts a night view of the
Center's entrance.

251

PROJECT
Desert Storm Memorial Competition
Kuwait City, Kuwait

ARCHITECT
HDS/Hans D. Strauch & Associates, Inc.
Boston, Massachusetts

RENDERING SIZE
9" x 12" (23 cm x 30 cm)

MEDIA
Conceptual sketch with felt-tip pen and
colored pencil

RIGHT
PROJECT
Waterfront Development Proposal

RENDERING SIZE
15" x 22" (38 cm x 56 cm)

MEDIA
Conceptual sketch with felt-tip pen and
watercolor wash

BELOW LEFT
PROJECT
Charter Oak Country Club
Hudson, Massachusetts

ARCHITECT
Fuller Associates, Inc.
Boston, Massachusetts

RENDERING SIZE
12" x 20" (30 cm x 51 cm)

MEDIUM
Watercolor

This is the view from putting green to
clubhouse.

BELOW RIGHT
PROJECT
Charter Oak Country Club
Hudson, Massachusetts

ARCHITECT
Fuller Associates, Inc.
Boston, Massachusetts

RENDERING SIZE
9" x 17" (23 cm x 43 cm)

MEDIUM
Watercolor

View of main entrance.

PROJECT
Back Bay,
Boston, Massachusetts

CLIENT
Self-commissioned

RENDERING SIZE
30" x 40" (76 cm x 102 cm)

MEDIUM
Graphite pencil on vellum

Courtesy of Mr. & Mrs. Paul J. Carroll, AIA

PROJECT
Monument Valley

ARCHITECT
Self-commissioned

RENDERING SIZE
16.5" x 28.5" (42 cm x 72 cm)

MEDIUM
Watercolor

BELOW RIGHT
PROJECT
Monument Valley

CLIENT
Self-commissioned

RENDERING SIZE
24" x 31" (61 cm x 79 cm)

MEDIUM
Watercolor

CLIENT
Self-commissioned

RENDERING SIZE
6" x 8.25" (15 cm x 21 cm)

MEDIUM
Wax-based, black colored pencil

PROFESSIONAL AFFILIATIONS

*Member, Advisory Council, and past president of
American Society of Architectural Perspectivists*

*Honorary member of Japan Architectural
Renderers Association*

Member of Design Communication Association

*Professor, Mount Ida College,
Newton, Massachusetts*

PROJECT
Puerto Rico Conservatory
San Juan, Puerto Rico

ARCHITECTS
Arquitectos Diaz
San Juan, Puerto Rico
Domenech Hicks & Krockmalnic, Architects,
P.S.C.
Boston, Massachusetts

RENDERING SIZE
9" x 12" (23 cm x 30 cm)

MEDIA
Samples of conceptual sketches
with watercolor

This was a competition-winning project.

FUJIO YOSHIDA

PERS-PLANNING   301, 4-7-11, ZUIKO   HIGASHIYODOGAWA-KU OSAKA 533-0005 JAPAN   011-81-6-6327-4947 TEL AND FAX

Fujio Yoshida had been engaged in design and supervision in an architect's office; however, when he first saw Helmut Jacoby's of works, he was inspired to draw in perspective. For about twenty years, this has been his preferred method of expression. In drawing perspectives and doing design, Yoshida enjoys studying the architect's works. He appreciates the challenge presented by superior design. Although computer-generated illustration has recently been given a lot of attention, Yoshida prefers drawing perspective by hand. The coloration he uses—pastel or airbrush—depends on the pen-and-ink drawing.

ABOVE
PROJECT
Natural Science Museum
Kongo Mount, Japan
CLIENT
Osaka Prefecture
ARCHITECT
Issiki Architects & Partners
RENDERING SIZE
13" x 19" (33 cm x 48 cm)
MEDIA
Pen and ink, watercolor, and airbrush

LEFT
PROJECT
Osaka Business Park Proposal
Osaka, Japan
ARCHITECT
Pers-Planning
RENDERING SIZE
31" x 23" (79 cm x 58 cm)
MEDIA
Pen and ink, watercolor, and airbrush

PROJECT
Osaka Business Park Proposal (Sunset)
Osaka, Japan

ARCHITECT
Pers-Planning

RENDERING SIZE
31" x 23" (79 cm x 58 cm)

MEDIA
Pen and ink, watercolor, and airbrush

RIGHT
PROJECT
Osaka Business Park Proposal (Aerial View)
Osaka, Japan

ARCHITECT
Pers-Planning

RENDERING SIZE
31" x 23" (79 cm x 58 cm)

MEDIA
Pen and ink, watercolor, and airbrush

256

PROJECT
Proposed Osaka Station Renewal (Sunset)
Osaka, Japan
CLIENT
JR. Nishinihon Railway Company
ARCHITECT
Pers-Planning
RENDERING SIZE
26" x 22" (66 cm x 56 cm)
MEDIA
Pen and ink, watercolor, and airbrush

PROJECT
Proposed Osaka Station Renewal (Aerial View)
Osaka, Japan

CLIENT
JR. Nishinihon Railway Company

ARCHITECT
Pers-Planning

RENDERING SIZE
22" x 27" (56 cm x 69 cm)

MEDIA
Pen and ink, watercolor, and airbrush

This illustration received the Award of Excellence in Architecture in Perspective 12.

RIGHT
PROJECT
Kobe Harbor Land Development
Kobe, Japan

CLIENT
Housing and City Planning Corporation

ARCHITECT
Sakakura Associates Architects & Engineers

RENDERING SIZE
28" x 24" (71 cm x 61 cm)

MEDIA
Pen and ink, watercolor, and airbrush

BELOW
PROJECT
Matabura City Hall
Osaka, Japan

CLIENT
Matubara City

ARCHITECT
Naito Architects & Engineers

RENDERING SIZE
16" x 25" (41 cm x 64 cm)

MEDIA
Pen and ink, watercolor, and airbrush

PROJECT
Seoul Project
Seoul, South Korea

ARCHITECT
Kosumio Sekkei Architects & Associates

RENDERING SIZE
17" x 12" (43 cm x 30 cm)

MEDIA
Pen and ink, watercolor, and airbrush

BELOW
PROJECT
Flower Wholesaler Market Project
Kyoto, Japan

CLIENT
GRUS Institute

ARCHITECT
Pers-Planning

RENDERING SIZE
15" x 23" (38 cm x 58 cm)

MEDIA
Pastel, watercolor, and colored pencil

PROJECT
Hotel Project
Osaka, Japan

CLIENT
Inose Real Estate Inc.

ARCHITECT
Kansai Civil Engineering & Architect Consultants

RENDERING SIZE
26" x 21" (66 cm x 53 cm)

MEDIA
Pastel and watercolor

PROJECT
Kamo Resort Project
Okayama, Japan

ARCHITECT
Ken Asai Architectural Research Inc.

RENDERING SIZE
18" x 26" (46 cm x 66 cm)

MEDIA
Pen and ink, watercolor, and airbrush

BELOW LEFT
PROJECT
OU—110—O Project
Osaka, Japan

ARCHITECT
Kansai Civil Engineering & Architect Consultants

RENDERING SIZE
28" x 21" (71 cm x 53 cm)

MEDIA
Pastel and watercolor

BELOW RIGHT
PROJECT
Golf Club Project
Ishikawa, Japan

CLIENT
Hi Yama Kousan

ARCHITECT
Pers-Planning

RENDERING SIZE
23" x 18" (58 cm x 46 cm)

MEDIA
Pastel and colored pencil

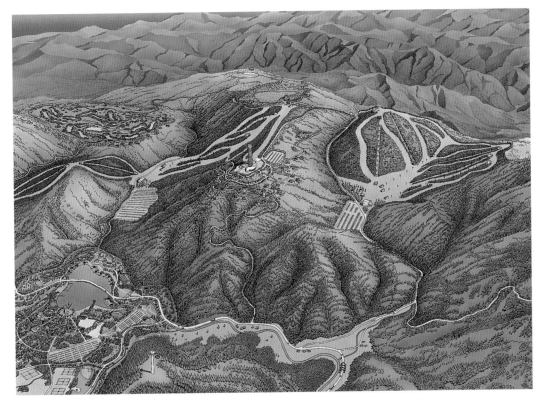

259

AARON K. ZIMMERMAN

WRSANIMATORS   120 NW PARKWAY   KANSAS CITY, MISSOURI 64150   816-587-9500 TEL   816-587-1685 FAX

Aaron Zimmerman began his illustration career after studying architecture and fine art at Kansas State University. He started using the computer to compose accurate perspective layouts and to have greater flexibility in view selection. These layouts would then be rendered in a variety of traditional media, including ink, colored pencil, marker, and watercolor. Now, after more than a decade of architectural and illustration experience, he leads WRSAnimators using the computer exclusively to produce architectural images of exceeding quality.

WRSAnimators works with various designers, architects, publishers, and inventors. With each client, the process evolves carefully with close attention paid to the target audience, artistic spirit, and design issues relevant to each project. The success of each rendering plays heavily in the subsequent success in securing public approval, investor confidence, and owner satisfaction. Therefore, with every image, WRSAnimators strives to achieve superior representation of design intent, mood, lighting, and context. To this end, WRSAnimators combines artistic talent with technical expertise to produce their award-winning architectural illustrations. WRSAnimators consists of three architectural artists and animators using the latest technology to produce works ranging from simple massing studies to highly articulate renderings and fully orchestrated architectural animation. WRSAnimators provides services including 3D modeling, visualization, animation, post-production, and wireframe generation.

ABOVE
PROJECT
Katewood Shores Retirement Center
Woodruff, Wisconsin
ARCHITECT
WRS Architects, Inc.
Kansas City, Missouri
RENDERING SIZE
14" x 25" (36 cm x 64 cm)
MEDIUM
Watercolor

This piece won the Award of Excellence in Architecture in Perspective 8.

LEFT
PROJECT
Tom Thomas Law Enforcement Center
Platte City, Missouri
ARCHITECT
WRS Architects, Inc.
Kansas City, Missouri
RENDERING SIZE
3,300 x 1,803 pixels
MEDIUM
Computer-generated

PROJECT
Wyndham Palmas Del Mar Resort and Villas
Humacao, Puerto Rico

ARCHITECT
WRS Architects, Inc.
Kansas City, Missouri

RENDERING SIZE
1,798 x 1,348 pixels

MEDIUM
Computer-generated

This piece won the Informal Category Award in
Architecture in Perspective 13.

PROJECT
The Monarch at Green Valley
Henderson, Nevada

ARCHITECT
WRS Architects, Inc.
Kansas City, Missouri

RENDERING SIZE
3,300 x 2,475 pixels

MEDIUM
Computer-generated

LEFT
PROJECT
The Monarch at Green Valley
Henderson, Nevada

ARCHITECT
WRS Architects, Inc.
Kansas City, Missouri

RENDERING SIZE
3,300 x 2,475 pixels

MEDIUM
Computer-generated

PROJECT
SAve a Connie Museum and
Aircraft Restoration Facility
Kansas City, Missouri

ARCHITECT
WRS Architects, Inc.
Kansas City, Missouri

RENDERING SIZE
5,400 x 4,050 pixels

MEDIUM
Computer-generated

This piece won the Award of Excellence in
Architecture in Perspective 12 and a Still Image
Award in *Architectural Record* (June 1997).

RIGHT
PROJECT
SAve a Connie Museum and
Aircraft Restoration Facility
Kansas City, Missouri

ARCHITECT
WRS Architects, Inc.
Kansas City, Missouri

RENDERING SIZE
5,400 x 3,634 pixels

MEDIUM
Computer-generated

BELOW RIGHT
PROJECT
SAve a Connie Museum and
Aircraft Restoration Facility
Kansas City, Missouri

ARCHITECT
WRS Architects, Inc.
Kansas City, Missouri

RENDERING SIZE
4,000 x 3,000 pixels

MEDIUM
Computer-generated

ABOVE LEFT

PROJECT
Marriott Residence Inn
Washington, DC

ARCHITECT
WRS Architects, Inc.
Kansas City, Missouri

RENDERING SIZE
1,444 x 1,069 pixels

MEDIUM
Computer-generated

ABOVE RIGHT

PROJECT
Marriott Residence Inn
Washington, DC

ARCHITECT
WRS Architects, Inc.
Kansas City, Missouri

RENDERING SIZE
1,444 x 1,069 pixels

MEDIUM
Computer-generated

LEFT

PROJECT
North American Sports Complex
Kansas City, Missouri

ARCHITECT
WRS Architects, Inc.
Kansas City, Missouri

RENDERING SIZE
5,400 x 3,095 pixels

MEDIUM
Computer-generated

BELOW LEFT

PROJECT
Las Palmas Doradas Condominiums and Hotel
Humacao, Puerto Rico

ARCHITECT
WRS Architects, Inc.
Kansas City, Missouri

RENDERING SIZE
4,300 x 2,850 pixels

MEDIUM
Computer-generated

This piece is by Greg Porter, WRSAnimators.

PROJECT
Center for Health in Aging
Kansas City, Kansas

ARCHITECT
WRS Architects, LLC
Overland Park, Kansas

RENDERING SIZE
5,400 x 3,095 pixels

MEDIUM
Computer-generated

RIGHT
PROJECT
Center for Health in Aging
Kansas City, Kansas

ARCHITECT
WRS Architects, LLC
Overland Park, Kansas

MEDIUM
5,400 x 3,811 pixels

MEDIUM
Computer-generated

Assistance on this piece was rendered by Greg
Porter, Neal Eidemiller, WRSAnimators.

PROFESSIONAL AFFILIATIONS

*Member, American Society of Architectural
Perspectivists*

RESOURCES

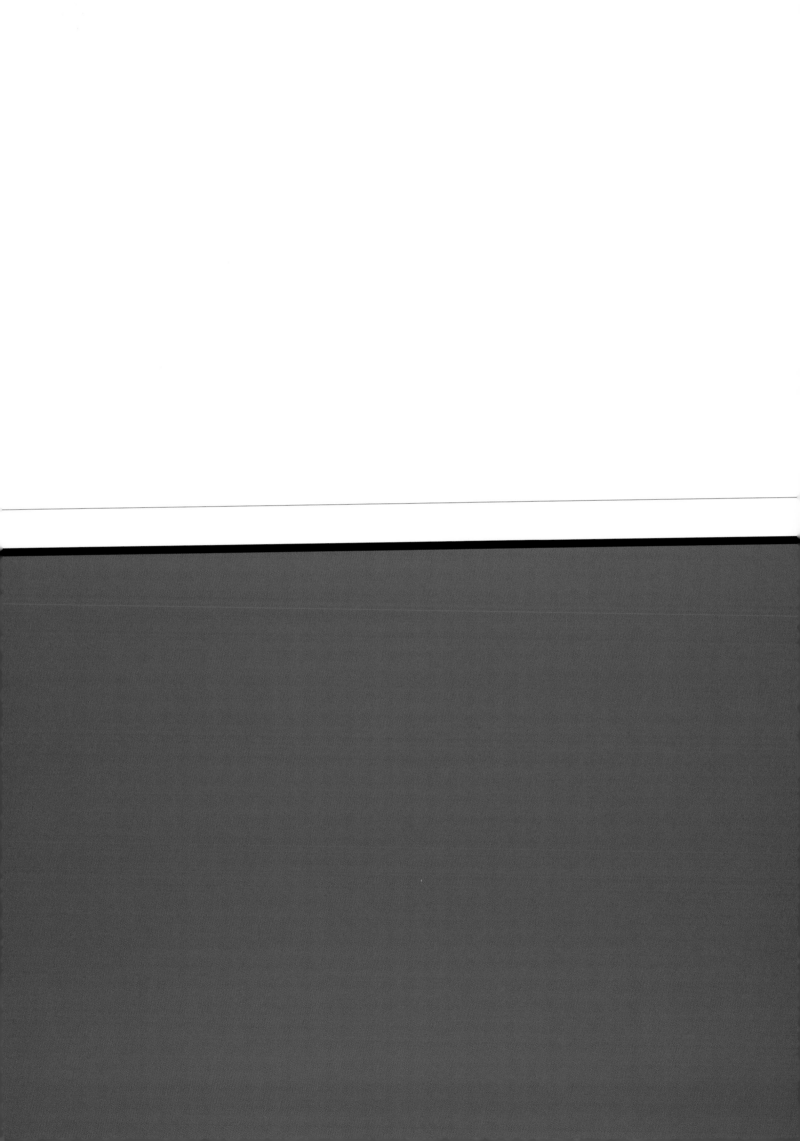

INDEX

SELECTED BIBLIOGRAPHY

269

The following list includes books that have been authored or edited by contributors to this volume, or books containing material submitted by them. The list is not comprehensive.

1. ASAP. *Architecture in Perspective.* New York: Van Nostrand Reinhold, 1992.
2. ASAP. *Architecture in Perspective [1–7].* Boston: ASAP, 1986–1992
3. ASAP. *Architecture in Perspective [8, 9].* San Francisco: Pomegranate Artbooks, 1993, 1994
4. Chen, John Li. *Architecture in Pen and Ink.* New York: McGraw-Hill Inc., 1995
5. Crowe, Philip. *Architecural Rendering.* Mies, Switzerland: Rotovision, 1991
6. Fraiha, Silvia, Designer. *A Arte De Illustrar A Arquitetura-Architectural Rendering Illustrated.* Rio De Janeiro, Brazil: Fraiha Editora, 1995
7. Grice, Gordon S., Ed. *Architecture in Perspective [10–12].* Rockport, Mass.: Rockport Publishers, 1995–1997
8. Grice, Gordon S., Ed. *Architecture in Perspective 13.* Sarasota, Fla.:Design Books International, Inc., 1998
9. Grice, Gordon S., Ed. *The Art of Architectural Illustration [1,2].* Rockport Mass.: Rockport Publishers, 1993, 1996
10. Korea Architectural Perspectivists Association. *Architectural Perspective.* Seoul, Korea: Architecture & the Environment, 1995
11. Pearlman/Stearns Inc. *Architectural Design Collaborators [1–3].* Natick, Mass.: Resource World Publications, Inc.

ACKNOWLEDGMENTS

The editor wishes to acknowledge the invaluable contribution of the following individuals to the preparation of this book:

Todd Crane, Don Fluckinger, Rosalie Grattarotti, Leeann Leftwich, Karen Norris, Stephen Perfetto, and Martha Wetherill of Rockport Publishers

Arthur Furst and Rob Pearlman of Resource World Publications

Tom Schaller, Frank Costantino, Steve Oles, and Barbara and Gary Ratner for their encouragement

Angelo de Castro, Willem van den Hoed, and David Xiaoping Xu for their willing and enlightened cooperation

Fanny Ghorayeb for her patience and support

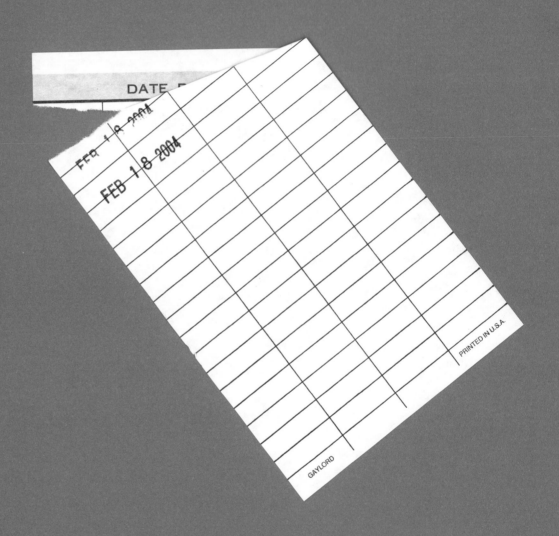

DATE

FEB 1 8 2004

FEB 1 8 2004

PRINTED IN U.S.A.

GAYLORD